ASIA
Traditions and Treasures

TITLE PAGE:
Minhab, a village in Iran

COPYRIGHT PAGE:
Cultivating rice in China; hand-colored lantern slide, c. 1925

CONTENTS PAGE:
Persepolis, capital of the ancient Persian Empire

PAGES 8-9:
Miyajima temple and its large torii, *or Shinto temple gateway, Japan;*
hand-colored lantern slide, c. 1925

PAGES 10—11
Floating market in Bangkok, Thailand

PAGES 12-13:
The Great Wall of China; hand-colored lantern slide, c. 1925

PAGES 14-15:
Mongolian village; hand-colored lantern slide, c. 1925

ENDPAPERS:
From A New General Atlas *by John Senex, London, 1721*

by WALTER A. FAIRSERVIS, JR.

Color photographs by Lee Boltin, Captions by Douglas J. Preston

ASIA TRADITIONS AND TREASURES

HARRY N. ABRAMS, Inc., *Publishers, New York*

In collaboration with the American Museum of Natural History

EDITORS: *Joan E. Fisher, Nora Beeson*   DESIGNER: *Philip Grushkin*

Illustrations © 1981 American Museum of Natural History

Published in 1981 by Harry N. Abrams, Incorporated, New York. All rights reserved. No part of the contents of this book may be reproduced without the written permission of the publishers

Printed and bound in Japan

Library of Congress Cataloging
in Publication Data
Fairservis, Walter Ashlin, 1921–
    Asia.

    Bibliography: p. 250
    Includes index.
    1. Asia—Civilization.
    2. Art—Asia.   I. Title.
DS12.F34   950   81-1814
ISBN 0-8109-0695-3   AACR2

CONTENTS

ACKNOWLEDGMENTS

The American Museum of Natural History gratefully acknowledges the help of numerous scholars who identified objects in the collection and provided information about the archival photographs:
Joan Aruz, Hagop Kevorkian Fellow, Ancient Near Eastern Art, Metropolitan Museum of Art; Robert Austerlitz, Professor, Uralic Studies, Columbia University; Sarah and Konrad Bekker; Richard W. Bulliet, Professor, Middle East Institute, Columbia University; Rand Castile, Director, Japan House Gallery; Myron A. Cohen, Professor, Department of Anthropology and East Asian Institute, Columbia University; Vaughn E. Crawford, Curator in Charge, Ancient Near Eastern Art, Metropolitan Museum of Art; Prudence O. Harper, Curator, Ancient Near Eastern Art, Metropolitan Museum of Art; Rabbi Philip Hiat, Union of American Hebrew Congregations; Marilyn Hirsh; Gari Ledyard, Professor, East Asian Languages and Cultures, Columbia University; Robert Mowry, Curator, Mr. and Mrs. John D. Rockefeller 3rd Collection, The Asia Society; Barbra Teri Okada, Consultant to the Japanese Collection, Newark Museum; Eleanora Ordjanian; S. Robert Ramsey, Jr., Assistant Professor, East Asian Languages and Cultures, Columbia University; William R. Roff, Professor, Southeast Asian History, Columbia University; Maureen Aung Thwin, Program Associate, The Asia Society; Richard Vinograd, Assistant Professor, Department of Art History and Archaeology, Columbia University; and the following staff members of the museum's Department of Anthropology: David Hurst Thomas, Barbara Conklin, Stanley A. Freed, Monna MacLellan, Harry L. Shapiro, Ian Tattersall, and Lisa Whittall. The museum would also like to thank the help of Bernice D'Aquino, Annlinn Grossman, Pamela Haas, A.A. Orth-Pallavicini, and Paula Perry for photographic research; Amy Halpern and Sue Gronewold for research assistance; Arthur Singer, James Coxe, and Peter Goldberg for photographic work; and Alan Ternes for editorial guidance. The museum would especially like to acknowledge the invaluable help of Douglas Preston; Cynthia Wilder in the museum's Department of Anthropology, who coordinated all the checking and rechecking of information about the photographs; at Harry N. Abrams, Nora Beeson for her work on the text, and Joan Fisher, who patiently directed the project.

*Color photography of the museum's Asian collection
was funded by the Henry Luce Foundation.*

FOREWORD

IT HAS BEEN ABOUT FOUR DECADES since that morning in Hawaii when American radios barked out the news that the Japanese had bombed Pearl Harbor. It is doubtful that given a map of the world half the American people of the day could have pointed to Japan, let alone to Pearl Harbor. A lesson was about to be taught that did not end with four years of hell of World War II. Names like Saipan, Okinawa, Iwo Jima, Nagasaki, and Hiroshima became part of American vocabulary, followed by Seoul, Kwangju, Pyong-yang, Inchon, and the Yalu. Americans found themselves fighting Koreans and Chinese, and Mao Tse-tung and Chou En-lai became names written in blood. From afar we saw the European empires in Asia dissolve, and heard the mass media describe the horrors of genocide on the Indian subcontinent as new nations arose there; we learned that a veteran French army was defeated by Vietnamese villagers in Tonkin, and that the Shah was thrown out of Iran only to return on the heels of a counterrevolution. Those seemed to be distant matters, but all of a sudden the American commitment in Asia became something more than mass-media chatter. The Burmese sent American missions packing; Jawaharlal Nehru of India refused American aid; and the pro-American governments in Southeast Asia proved unstable. More and more Americans were drawn into Vietnam until an undeclared full-scale war was launched against villagers who valued their own independence over the consequences of foreign victory. New names became familiar: Field of Jars, Hue, Da Nang, Saigon, and the Mekong Delta—add Cambodia and the Laotians. The consequences of an eventual peace agreement included the genocide of the Khmers and the aimless wandering of the Boat People.

Nor does it end there. The Near East joined the rest of Asia when the Israeli people fought for their state against the Arabs, who in turn controlled the oil vital to American industry. The Shah fled from Iran, the successful rebels seized American hostages, and names like Riyadh, Teheran, Shiraz, Ayatollah, Imam, Sheikh, Abu Dhabi, and Jedda join older Asian words in the American vocabulary.

Russia's Peter the Great (1682–1725) made his boyar nobility shave off their beards and wear European clothes. He opened a seaport on the Baltic and forcibly made Russia face west. During the Enlightenment, Catherine the Great corresponded with Voltaire as her elite gazed toward France from beneath Byzantine onion domes. Throughout the last two hundred years Russian intelligentsia has sought to spread Western thought, but czars and commissars turned the Russian people toward their natural perspective—east. Possessing the vast interior of the Eurasian continent, with lands open to the Central Asian passageways toward Cathay, Russia is more intimate with Kirghiz, Kazakh, Uzbek, and Tatar peoples than with French or Germans in spite of historical connections with both. Russia is more Asian than European in most of its culture. The United States and Russia are at continued odds, and such names as Moscow, Leningrad, Sverdlovsk, Odessa, and Kiev have become commonplace in America, as now are Kabul and the Khyber Pass, owing to Russia's move into Afghanistan.

Surely anyone reading the above with any degree of objectivity would have to comment that something is wrong. Either Americans know what they are doing in Asia or they do not. The answer has to be the latter. But why is this so? In spite of massive government grants to institutions of learning for programs in Asian studies, in spite of foreign service, in spite of modern ease of travel, the United States still comes up with simplistic material approaches based on economic and social determinism. Our understanding of Asia is patronizing and chauvinistic. Our image of Asia remains virtually unchanged since Marco Polo's day when his account of the exotic East tickled his Venetian audience's fancy. The images are stereotypic: tong wars, Fu Manchu, Charlie Chan, the Dragon Lady, Bruce Lee, Douglas Fairbanks as Sinbad, and more recently the British movie "Death of a Princess," in which is shown Asian cruelty to titillate and fulfill the exotic requirement. There is an anger in Asia at Americans that in many ways is far more emotional today than in the days of colonial dominance.

There is a presumption, actually an arrogance, in many Westerners' writing about the life and values of another people. As I point out later on, it is our Western way to think that the ability to objectify and analyze will provide understanding. The pages of many a learned journal devoted to Asia do assume just that, as does the pedantic language in many textbooks. It is our way of doing things.

The focus of my text is on traditional Asia and the fine photographs taken by my compatriot Lee Boltin are also a help in understanding the traditional life of Asian peoples. It is not intended for the photographs or the text to be a complete representation of Asia; rather, this book presents a sampling of some of the finest offerings that have been collected by the museum over the years. Because I have spent most of my life studying and living among Asian peoples from Japan to the Mediterranean, and the past twelve years working on the most comprehensive exhibit on Asian peoples in the New World, the Hall of Asian Peoples in the American Museum of Natural History, I am certainly aware more than most of the immense need for insight. I have to confess a love of Asians wherever they come from that amounts to more than affection or emotional awe of their accomplishments. It arises from a sense of brotherhood, one that has many dimensions in so many realms of the mind. For when one thinks of the far horizons of the geographic earth, an Asian traveler is there to offer hospitality.

I have to leave out of this writing the undeniable fact that the highroads of Asia have long offered personal, exotic, pleasurable moments. But surely, Asians too love the smells of their spiced food; the heavy perfumes of tropical gardens; the music of native traditions; the awesome temples and palaces; the delicacy of fine craftsmanship; the compelling vulgarity of raw color; the supernatural intricacy of calligraphy; the myriad peoples who throng for whatever reason; the mightiness of mountain, desert, or river; and perhaps above all, the poetry, the literature of today and yesterday. Since we cannot recreate here the experience of the Asian highroads, the photographs of the objects so painstakingly gathered over the last hundred years by American Museum of Natural History scientists, travelers, and friends must convey a flavor that, once tasted, stays with the spirit and motivates return. It is in this constant motivation to return that the answer to our lack of understanding of Asia may be found. For Asia is no way-stop on a road to somewhere else. It is the most substantial symbol of man's capability of comprehending his place in nature. It is in Asia that the two ways of comprehension are found: to reason with one's intellect, to experience with one's spirit through faith.

A thatched house in rural Thailand is a background for a pool with waterlilies. Surrounding the house are rice fields. Thailand is a picturesque country characterized by deciduous and coniferous forests, upland regions intersected by rivers, mountain ranges, and undulating forested plateaus. (Orme, recent)

I

ASIA—THE GEOGRAPHICAL PREMISE

ASIA IS THE LARGEST CONTINENT on the face of the earth. It has the world's largest populations, the highest mountains, the most diverse cultures. All of man's great religions originated in Asia; it is the seat of the world's earliest as well as the most long-lived civilizations. In Asia began the first writing system, the first alphabets, the first metallurgy. Here also was the first domestication of plants and animals, and the beginning of settled life based on food production. To Asia we owe the first irrigation systems, the principle of the wheel, the earliest cities, the first codified law, and the Ten Commandments. Here began philosophy and the science of astronomy. The fountain of Asian accomplishment has flowed unceasingly since the appearance of modern man in the midst of the dynamism of the Pleistocene Age.

Henry Fairfield Osborn, former president of the American Museum of Natural History in New York, used the term Mother Asia not simply as a statement of Asiatic man's accomplishment; flushed by scientific discovery in Central Asia of the evidence for primeval life, he could not help but envision a primordial earth mother. Ellsworth Huntingdon, an outstanding and intrepid geographer who traveled over much of the continent, spoke of the pulse of Asia, by which he meant climatic cycles that sent pastoral peoples seeking new pastures and often brought about the invasion of old civilizations in their path, thus changing the course of history. How many Europeans and Americans came to Asia and were profoundly changed by its character: Lawrence of Arabia, Marco Polo, Henry Lawrence, Lafcadio Hearn, Thomas Merton, and countless others. Such change comes about because immersion into Asian life touches upon the inner dynamism that has made Asia paramount in human history.

Today, with Asia so drastically different even from the days of Osborn and Huntingdon, it is hard to envision an older Asia of tradition, but it is not so strange, viewed from the context of time, that Americans are greatly influenced by Asia for better or for worse. Americans have made Asia a battlefield, a source of raw materials, and a market for products. American political life is colored by events in Asia, and American families all too often mourn lost members dead somewhere in Asia. American shops sell Asian products that are often better made than their own. Asia is vital to Western man for resources, for other views, indeed for dreams.

What then is this Asia? Initially it is a landmass in the eastern hemisphere, so vast that it makes Europe a mere peninsula. From Aden on the southeastern corner of Arabia to the Bering Strait, it is 6,500 miles, and over 4,000 miles from Cape Comorin on the tip of the Indian subcontinent to the Poluostrov peninsula on the Arctic Ocean. It is 3,800 miles from Baghdad to Peking as the crow flies. But for land travel one must add at least half that distance to the total mileage, for the roads go only where mountain pass and oasis allow. In the days of the Mongol Kublai Khan, with good horses it was possible to make

Camels rest with their burdens at a principal caravan terminus at the former British colony of Aden, now a part of Yemen. Aden has the only good harbor between Egypt and Iran on the Red Sea, and has been a major port and caravan terminus for centuries.

An ancient, fortified city gate of Kashgar gives some idea of the defense system this city once possessed; it was a major trading center on an ancient trade route running through Central Asia. (W. J. Morden, 1920s)

the journey in less than five months. Traveling by sea, resting upon the vagaries of wind and current, would take perhaps six to nine months to reach ports nearest to those famous cities. Voyages of several years could be expected for any long trip no matter how the crow flies. This is why the way stations on the old roads achieved such fame: Lanchow, Tun-huang, Khotan, Kashgar, Taliqan, Tashkurghan, ancient Merv, Bamian, Peshawar . . . literally all caravanserais en route to somewhere else. They were places where rest and refreshment could be had, gossip and story could be exchanged as caravans wended their way to the great emporium cities of the East, West, and South. The caravanserai is for many the true symbol of Asia, for in spite of the continent's vast seacoasts most Asians are land-oriented.

Neither the Indians, Japanese, nor Chinese were early seafarers, and it was not until late in the history of the latter two that sea travel became important. It was the Koreans, however, who braved the seas of China and Japan conveying merchandise and monks between the two countries. Similarly, Indonesian and Malay sailors were often the ones who brought Indians and their produce to Southeast Asia. But only the Arabs in western Asia made seafaring a critical part of their activity. Arab dhows reached Canton and traded as early as the eighth century A.D., and their ancestors conveyed the trade of Rome to India. A Roman seaport has been found at Arikamedo, near Pondicherry on the Bay of Bengal, where Roman pottery has been unearthed that was almost certainly brought by Arab intermediaries from the Roman ports on the Red Sea.

For most Asians it is the land routes that count. The Chinese looked beyond the Great Wall to the Turkestan roads via Dzungaria, the Indians looked to the Khyber and Gomel passes, and the Persians to the northern roads from Turkestan to the Caucasus

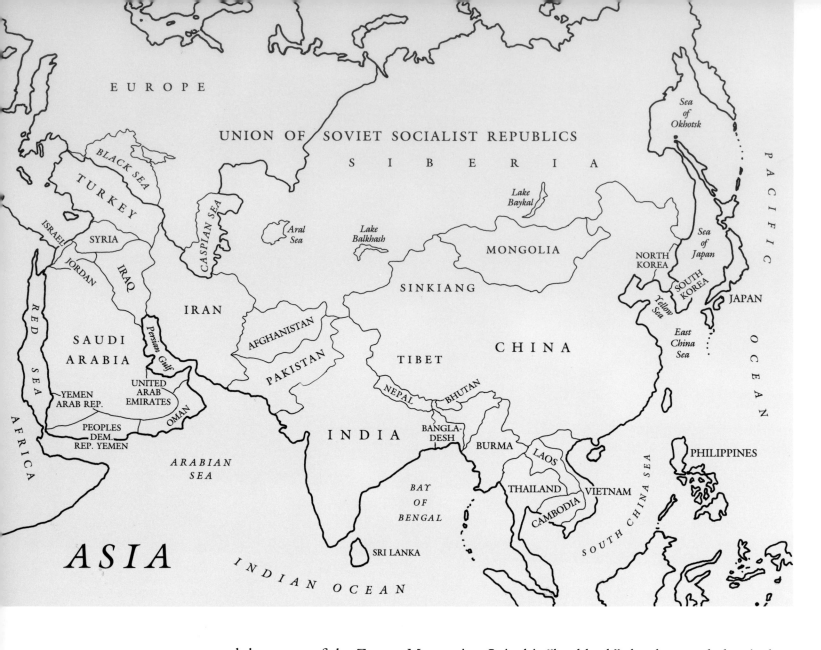

ASIA

and the passes of the Zagros Mountains. It is this "land look" that has tended to isolate Asians from one another. Land borders are very important, not simply as markers of territories but because the people within those borders have vehement feelings about their own lands. For a Chinese to have to travel abroad was a risk, for he wanted to be born and buried in the homeland of his ancestors. China, Korea, Burma, Thailand, Tibet, and Japan have all at one time or another followed policies of isolationism not just to keep foreign influences out, but more strikingly to express an inner devotion to the homeland, where all that was necessary for human happiness in this life could be found. This is one of the most difficult concepts for the Westerner to realize. The West has done all it can do to destroy isolationism, yet often that very isolationism gave the country involved a securer hold on its own traditions and, as a consequence, a more harmonious life for its people. Today, this question is endlessly debated in many Asian countries: Burma refuses any effective contact with the West; China wrestles with an essentially Chinese effort to make Marxism Chinese; Yukio Mishima committed public suicide to protest Japan's overcommitment to what he conceived of as a destructive Westernization; even India, long under the British, attempts to isolate itself from world entanglements. This debate is

Between 1915 and 1930, Roy Chapman Andrews conceived, organized, and led a series of museum expeditions to Central Asia, where he hoped to find the birthplace of the human race. One hundred and twenty-five camels (pictured here) carried the expedition's food, water, and gasoline; the expedition members traveled by motor car. They traversed thousands of miles of the vast Gobi Desert, collecting fossils, rocks, flora, fauna, archeological remains, ethnographic material, and just about anything else of scientific interest. (J.B. Shackelford, 1928)

The camel was a very useful animal to the nomadic Mongols. Aside from being able to go for long periods without water and food, camels supplied hair for high-quality felt.

The Caucasus mountain range is the homeland for more than fifty separate peoples, each speaking its own language. The diversity can be traced back at least to Roman times, when Pliny the Elder wrote that the Romans needed eighty interpreters to do business there. This photograph shows a group of Caucasian dancers with castanets for accompaniment.

Two Georgians pose for this studio photograph, wearing the traditional costume of their region: a long wool coat with bullet pouches, straight short sword, silk shirt, and baggy trousers tucked into high boots. The dress shows Iranian, Turkish, and Ukrainian influences, and was well suited for riding. (late 19th or early 20th century)

These women in a Shan market are from the eastern hill country of Burma on the border of Chinese Yunnan. They wear the Shan wickerwork hats and Burmese blouses with lungis *(skirts)*.

not just confined to Asian countries, for Asians in the United States are also challenged by it. One of the contemporary conflicts within the Chinatowns is between the established Chinese who want to retain the old, largely Confucian values that once gave the Chinese community its cohesiveness and that tended to isolate the Chinese from other American communities, and the new generation of Chinese, backed by recent immigrants, who want to be part of the American mainstream and receive all its benefits.

Asia lends itself to isolation, not only because of its great size but also the particular way it is divided by mountains and deserts. Starting in the west in Anatolia, modern Turkey, a country of mountains and hills surrounding an inner plateau and possessing a narrow seacoast that is studded with inlets and small islands (the old Ionia of the Greeks), Anatolia reaches to Europe and the Balkans at the Dardanelles. Eastward, it merges with the Caucasus and the mountain countries of Armenia, Georgia, and Azerbaijan. The Caucasus has always been a land of isolated, fiercely independent people who fought off Russians, Persians, and Turks through the centuries to preserve their way of life. It is no coincidence that the Armenian form of Christianity is among the oldest of that faith, nor that Mount Ararat is an Armenian symbol.

Two great mountain chains branch out of this region. The Elburz, which forms the barrier between the Caspian Sea region and the desert of Persia, and the Zagros of western Iran, which in southwestern Iran pivot eastward, running then as coastal ranges some 1,200 miles to the valley of the Indus River in modern Pakistan. This makes Iran essentially a land of interior drainage as is its eastern neighbor, Afghanistan. Since the rainfall in these regions is sparse, less than ten inches per year much of the time, the areas in or close to the mountains, where the runoff collects, are the most fertile. It is here that the cities Isfahan, Teheran, Shiraz, Meshed, Herat, and Kandahar are located; they are centers of Iranian culture. In the western mountains, the isolation is broken by pastoral nomadic groups who, like the peoples of the Caucasus, are fiercely independent. Noteworthy among those groups are the Kurds, who still struggle for a separate nation.

West of the great plateau of Iran are the Semitic-language countries of the Arabs and Hebrews. The great massif of Arabia is made up of ancient rocks and more recent marine deposits in which are found the oil reserves that have given the region such prominence today. Until recently the Arabian peninsula has been the home of the bedouin, the desert pastoral nomad whose mobility with camel and horse permits seasonal movement over wide areas. The highest mountains of Arabia are in the west along the Red Sea coasts of Hejaz and Yemen. From northern Arabia there is a gentle slope eastward to the great alluvial trough of the Tigris and Euphrates rivers, the ancient fertile alluvial plain with Babylon-Baghdad at its center. This region with the Levant, the countries of the eastern Mediterranean, was the center of several great Islamic empires, like those of the Umayyads of Damascus and Abbasids of Baghdad.

The Yalu River forms the boundary between Manchuria and Korea. A slender boat ferries horses and goods across a branch of the Yalu. (Roy Chapman Andrews, 1911–12)

Korean farmers sometimes use seaweed as a fertilizer. It is collected partly decayed above the high-tide mark; here it is carried back to the field. (Roy Chapman Andrews, 1912)

The Levant consists of a series of moderately high hill ranges rising from and parallel to the fertile Mediterranean coast, with each successive range receiving less and less rainfall. In the Jordan River trough, desert conditions ensue, and then surprisingly there is more rainfall eastward along the higher ranges of Jordan, one mountain of which, Mount Nebo, was where Moses at last saw the land of Canaan.

The highest mountains in the world almost entirely cut off the Indo-Pakistan subcontinent from the rest of Asia. The Himalaya-Karakorum-Hindu Kush ranges are formidable barriers to north-south travel. On the west the lower Sulaiman range, which marks the eastern rim of the Iranian plateau, is pierced by passes whose rivers debouch onto the Indus plain, and only here is access reasonably possible. This region is a tribal area occupied by the Baluch, Brahui, and Pathans. The Pathans are a dominant people in Afghanistan and along the Pakistan side of the northwest frontier, and, though fractionalized by tribalism, they are another proud, individual people with a hybridization of culture representative of their borderland situation.

India consists of three great physiographic parts. The central plateau is called the Deccan, which consists of ancient rocks thrust up and tilted from west to east causing most south Indian rivers to drain eastward. Between this plateau and the great mountain chains on the north and west is a deep trough which is filled with the sediments eroded from the mountains by the Indus and Ganges rivers and their tributaries. This sediment-filled region is the most fertile area in India-Pakistan and here are the heaviest populations and the largest native cities: Lahore, Amritsar, Delhi, Lucknow, Allahabad, Patna, Benares. The seacoasts and adjacent coastal ranges are also centers of population, particularly where the Dravidian-speaking Tamil and Telugu groups practice an intensive rice agriculture.

Rice mills like this one in Korea were common throughout the East wherever rice was grown. Milling removes the hull and bran layers from the kernel of rice. No part of the rice is wasted during the milling process: broken kernels are used to make rice wine and rice flour, hulls are used for fuel, bran is processed for oil, and the rice straw is used for feed, livestock bedding, thatch, mats, brooms, and even raincoats, hats, and snow boots. (Roy Chapman Andrews, 1912)

By its geography India is divided quite neatly. Tribal people live in the isolated zones of mountain valleys, jungles, or deserts, while the Deccan helps to separate south Indian groups from the northern groups. Since the northern area is directly accessible to the west, it has historically received outside influences to a much greater extent than the more isolated and conservative south. This isolation was not broken until the advent of European sea power in the sixteenth century.

Southeast Asia is largely a region of hills, mountains, and alluvial plains. Most of the rivers flow almost due south between steep mountains and prominent hills. The richest regions for agriculture are therefore in the delta zones. Because of the rugged terrain in Southeast Asia, east-west travel has always been difficult, as was apparent to Allied Forces moving into Burma in World War II. Possession of the great delta regions has long had political ramifications, for these deltas are the foundation for old civilizations as well as for modern nations. The Vietnamese seizure of the Mekong River delta is now but a historical verity, painful as it may be.

The hills of Southeast Asia are inhabited by a bewildering number of tribal groups, many of whom have ethnic ties to tribal groups in Southwest China, such as the Yao and Hmong. These tribes and the sedentary Thai, Khmer, and Burmese have usually lived together symbiotically, trading raw materials for manufactured ones or exchanging one

A Korean farmer and his daughter stand in front of their yellow-clay house with a thatched roof. Korea, as the physical and cultural bridge between North China and Japan, shows a mixture of both cultures combined with strong indigenous roots. Koreans lived close to the soil and farmed with simple wooden plows and hoes. (Roy Chapman Andrews, 1912)

Mongolia is one of the richest fossil-bearing areas in the world. This view looking north of Tiger Canyon in the Tsagan Nor Basin shows the arid and eroded topography of the Gobi Desert, which covers much of Mongolia. The Central Asiatic Expedition found abundant fossils of deer, ostrich, mastodon, and horse, indicating that the region was once fertile. (J.B. Shackelford, 1925)

OPPOSITE:

In Tibetan Buddhist belief, deities called the dharmapala *(Guardians of the Faith) assume terrible and frightening aspects to subdue the enemies of the faithful. Depicted here is a gilt bronze figure of Yamāntaka, the conqueror of the Lord of Death (Yama), who tried to depopulate Tibet in his insatiable search for victims. The* dharmapala *are often depicted with crowns of skulls, flayed human skins, human skull cups filled with blood, and belts of severed human heads. According to the Tibetan Book of the Dead, by having meditated during life on these "blood-drinking" deities, a person may recognize them after death, and not be frightened by them or distracted from the path toward a better reincarnation. Height: 18 inches*

A Hmong girl hauls water in bamboo tubes. The Hmong is a tribal group of northern Laos who inhabits mainly the upper slopes and mountaintops of the country. They are related to similar peoples living across the border in Thailand and China. Some are animists and others Buddhists, often with strong Confucian influences. (J. Halpern, c. 1960)

foodstuff for another. The tribal people, like so many other mountain people in Asia, jealously guard and retain their ethnic traditions in spite of contacts with the sedentary civilizations of the lowlands. This is as true for the Naga of Burma as for the Shan tribes on Burma's China frontier, the Montagnards of Vietnam, and the numerous tribes of Laos. To the south, in the Malay peninsula, dense jungles are the homeland for the aboriginal Semai, who still retain their old traditions while coming into contact with the "progressive" Malays whose far-ranging sea voyages made them international in outlook.

The mountain Muztagh Ata, at the heart of the Pamir of Central Asia, has sometimes been called the "navel of the world." Indeed, for the world of Asia it has special significance, for it marks the division between western and eastern Asia and is the turning point for the people of Central Asia. Westward are the broad, open plains and deserts of Turkestan, while eastward are the Altai Mountains and the inner deserts of high and low Central Asia. Beyond the Himalayas is the high plateau of Tibet—a region of vastness where pastoral nomads function in elevations above twelve thousand feet, while down in the valleys Tibetan farmers cultivate the limited soil for their tsamba and barley. Tibet is a region of isolation—an immense, high, generally barren plateau between two great moun-

(text continued on page 41)

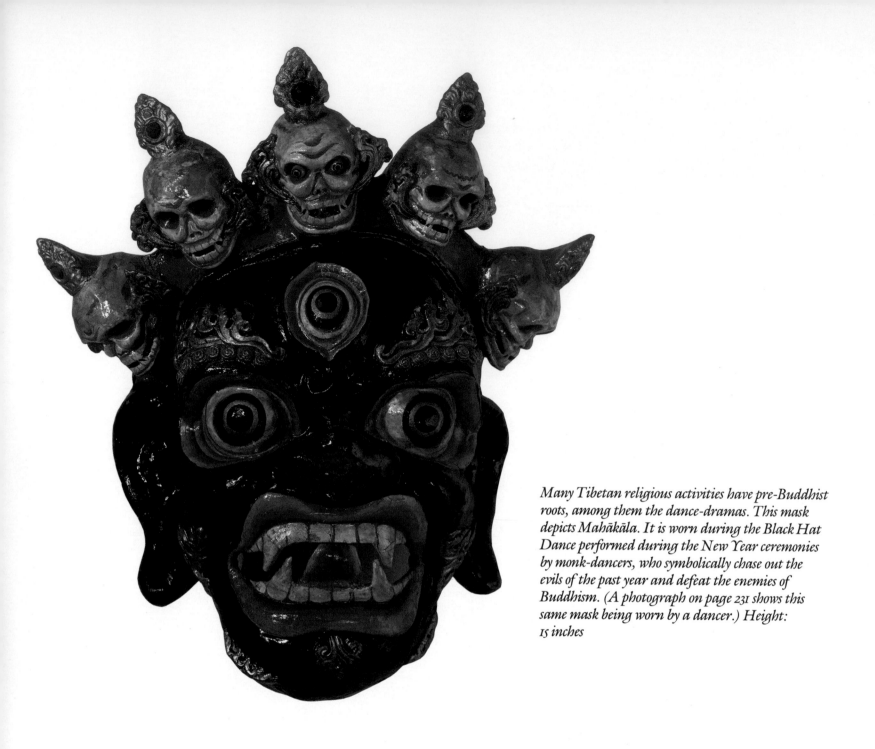

Many Tibetan religious activities have pre-Buddhist roots, among them the dance-dramas. This mask depicts Mahākāla. It is worn during the Black Hat Dance performed during the New Year ceremonies by monk-dancers, who symbolically chase out the evils of the past year and defeat the enemies of Buddhism. (A photograph on page 231 shows this same mask being worn by a dancer.) Height: 15 inches

OPPOSITE:

Aprons of carved human bone were worn by monks in Tibet, chiefly during the New Year dance ceremonies of exorcising the past year's evils. Height: 31 inches

OPPOSITE:

An Indian teacher, Padmasambhava, depicted in this tangka, or religious painting, is revered for bringing Buddhism from India to Tibet in the eighth century. Called "precious teacher," he popularized the new faith by adding to it pre-Buddhist Tibetan gods and spirits. He established the first monastery in Tibet in 749 A.D. The tangka is painted with water-soluable vegetable and mineral pigments on linen treated with chalk and glue. Height: 25 inches

The Wheel of Transmigratory Existence depicts symbolically the Tibetan view of reincarnation. All beings are trapped in a cycle of death and rebirth from which they can be liberated only by reaching spiritual enlightenment. The six sections of the wheel show the six realms of rebirth (clockwise from top): gods, demigods, tortured spirits, hells, animals, and humans. The pig, cock, and snake at the wheel's hub symbolize the three basic poisons that bind people to earth: ignorance, desire, and hatred, respectively. The symbols around the outer rim show the twelve conditions in life that bind people to rebirth, e.g., a man plucking fruit (clinging to worldly things); two men in a boat (mind and body); empty houses with windows (the six senses); and lovers (sensual contact). Height: 37 inches

The dance-dramas sponsored by the monasteries draw upon the rich tradition of history, legend, and myth of Tibetan Buddhism. The masked dances are sometimes satirical, mocking such things as love and the nobility. This deer mask is worn during a dance that tells the story of a teacher, Milarepa, who saves a frightened stag from a hunter and through songs of kindness and compassion converts the hunter to a better way of life. Height: 14 inches

OPPOSITE:

Buddhism was already twelve hundred years old when it arrived in Tibet, and brought with it a large number of deities. Some native Tibetan gods were added to the new religion, which resulted in a complex pantheon of several thousand deities and saints in Tibet. Shown here are animal-headed Makaravaktrā (left), and Vasantadevi, a goddess of the four seasons (right); both are attendants of the goddess Śrīdevī, called Lhamo by Tibetans. Height: (left) 8½ inches; (right) 6¼ inches

(text continued from page 32)

tain ranges: the Himalaya-Karakorum to the south and west, and the Kunlun on the north. Beyond the Kunlun, in the land the Chinese call Sinkiang, the terrain sharply drops into the basin of the feeble Tarim River. Here the roads press close to the bases of the mountains and go from oasis to oasis east and west on both sides of the Tarim basin. On the north edge of the basin are the Mountains of Heaven, the Tien Shan, the border range between the desert of Central Asia and the steppe and forestlands to the north. This Sinkiang is a rainless and difficult land—bitter cold in winter, burning hot in summer. Yet in it live Kirghiz and Uighur Muslims, who are both sedentary and nomadic, and through it have gone the caravans and pilgrims of the old silk roads, seeking the markets and sanctuaries of India and China—and indeed of the Mediterranean. Roman coins have been found here, and it is recorded that the Roman emperor Tiberius passed an edict forbidding Roman gold to be paid for the silk of the East.

North of the Tien Shan is a broad, open plain—a gap between the Mountains of Heaven and the northern Altai, the forested slopes of which are filled with tales and legends told by the pastoral nomadic Turkic and Mongol peoples of Genghis Khan and of the Seven Yak Tails banner. This gap is known as the Dzungarian Gates and is the road for the hordes of pastoral nomads such as the Turks, Mongols, and Huns, who in their movement westward changed the course of history. Eastward, pastureland merges into the sullen aridity of the Gobi desertlands. Here the Roy Chapman Andrews expeditions found the famed dinosaur eggs and much other paleontological information. The Gobi extends far to the east, reaching to the Great Wall and the basin of the Yellow River and farther east into the heart of Manchuria. It is a bridgeland and a barrier according to the vagaries of its seasons.

Manchuria is bordered on the north by the Amur River in the midst of a mixed forest of coniferous and deciduous trees. Here the Goldi and Gilyak live on the abundant fish and game, making their Chinese-style clothing from salmon skin, while following the essential shamanistic ideologies of Siberia. Traditionally living in the center of Manchuria were horsemen, pastoral nomads of Gobi type, who mingled with eastern and southern farmers, many of whom were invading Chinese, a situation not unlike in Korea to the southeast.

Korea extends out of the south and east of Manchuria, divided from that land by the Yalu River and from the rest of Asia by the Yellow and Japan Seas. Ranging in length through some eleven degrees of latitude, with an interior mountain range along the central and eastern sides, Korea has a nearly tropical environment among its myriad islands in the south, a Siberian climate in the north, and almost every other climate between. In the west and south, rice agriculture is excellent; in the north, lumbering and millet are staples. It is two lands bound in one.

Mahākāla, "The Great Black One," is a dharmapala, one of the Guardians of the Faith of Buddhism. He is shown here dark blue in color. In some of his many forms Mahākāla is the protector of the tent and of science. He is also one of the deities associated with the Black Hat Dance performed at New Year ceremonies. Height: 13½ inches

The Yukaghir summer tent resembles the teepee of the American Indian and consists of a framework of poles covered with skins. (probably Waldemar Borgoras, c. 1900)

The Morden-Clark Expedition of the American Museum crossed Mintaka Pass in the spring of 1926 with the aid of bearers and yaks. Mintaka Pass (15,500 feet), aside from harboring the rare snow leopard, is today a unique spot politically because it is located on the border of Pakistan, China, Russia, and Afghanistan; it is also at the convergence of three great mountain ranges: the Karakorum, Pamir, and Hindu Kush. (J.L. Clark, 1926)

The Manchurian and Korean reaches into a Siberian environment are also duplicated in Japan. But Japan, on the eastern extreme of the Asian continent, extends even farther north and south. Made up essentially of four main islands, it covers more than twenty degrees of latitude. There are Southeast Asian features in Japan, including pole houses, rice cultivation, and certain legends; on the other hand, there are also Central Asian features, such as horses, certain weapons, yet other legends, and there are the Ainu, whose language and cultural affinities are closer to those of the Siberian peoples than anyone else in Asia. The Japanese historically leaned heavily on China for certain prime parts of their culture. Thus with a powerful indigenous ethos Japan has amalgamated many elements normally alien to it and produced the classic culture we know as Japanese. This has been accomplished in spite of a land of which less than 15 percent is cultivable and one that is isolated by the sea from the rest of Asia. It is also a land of earthquake and typhoon. Its holy mountain Fuji is a volcano from which some say smoke emerges from time to time as if warning of apocalypse.

North of the Altai Mountains and the Amur River is the vastness of forest, river, and lake known as Siberia. Here most of the rivers flow to the Arctic Ocean over flat taiga and tundra lands. There are mountains in the northeast corner of Siberia and on Kamchatka up to the Bering Sea. It is a bitter-cold, seemingly endless world in which reindeer-dependent tribes, such as the Chukchi and Koryak in the northeast, and the Kamchadal, Lamut, Yukaghir, and Tungus of central and northern Siberia, had various ways of using the animal. Exceptional in their horse- and cattle-keeping were the Turkic-speaking Yakut of central Siberia, who, like their distant relatives the Ottoman Turks of Anatolia, moved out of Central Asia a millennium or more ago. All of these people are shamanistic and subject to the phenomenon common in remote and rugged regions

A Reindeer Koryak boy steadies a newborn reindeer calf. When the calf is older it will pull Koryak sleds from herding areas in the interior mountains to the winter camps on the Sea of Okhotsk. (Waldemar Jochelson, 1900)

known as arctic hysteria. Their adaptation to what is one of the most challenging and formidable climates in the world is marvelous proof of the natural selectivity of man—a statement of man's endurance in the midst of organic life.

China is of course the heart of eastern Asia. It is the most influential and largest culture area in Asia proper. China is geographically two fundamentally different regions: North China, centered on the alluvial plain of the Yellow (Huang Ho) River; and South China, which is a generally mountainous region south of the Yangtze (Ch'ang Chiang) River. North China has temperate climate and grows millet, barley, and some rice. South China is a rice-growing area, especially in the tropical coastal and inland basins and river valleys. Climate around Canton is monsoonal and tropical. Peking on the other hand is temperate and often dust-covered from the loess swept in off the Gobi.

The Chinese generally moved south from their prehistoric homeland established in North China. But their population, over one billion, has consumed the landscape. From more than two hundred million people in the eighteenth century, the Chinese have grown almost five times in number. Only intensive agricultural practice can save the Chinese from a disastrous starvation—something already anticipated, it would seem, in the Confucian emphasis on cultivating the land from one generation to the next.

Thus Asia in its broad geographical structure provides for, and indeed insists on, regions of isolation and regions of heavy concentration, the latter being connected despite wide separation from one another by another kind of region—the bridgeland. In defining the setting of Asia's cultures and their ethnohistorical substance, these three basic premises—bridgelands, regions of isolation, regions of concentration—must be understood, for whether or not a culture is located in one or another of them has a great deal to do with its character.

Although Russian traders had penetrated Siberia in the seventeenth and eighteenth centuries, it was not until the nineteenth century that the Russians conquered and dominated the region. The Russians brought Western goods, disease, and Christianity; here, a Russian Orthodox priest in deerskins stands with rifle in hand at Gishiga, on the Sea of Okhotsk. (N.G. Buxton, 1901)

II

THE ORIGIN
OF ASIAN
CIVILIZATION

IT IS APPARENT THAT ASIA was not the location for the origin of man, but did have a role in man's later development. The place of origin appears to be Africa, as evidenced by numerous finds of the upright primate Australopithecus and his tools, which are basically pebbles with flakes knocked off as a consequence of battering or of rudimentary efforts to form a chopping or cutting edge. Such pebbles, however, are also known from early Pleistocene deposits in England, Belgium, Kashmir, and Israel, so it is conceivable that forms of Australopithecus existed in a wider distribution than Africa, but this is by no means certain. In the Siwalik hills of Pakistan a number of fossil primates of Miocene-Pliocene age have been found, some of which may be in the ancestral line toward man. One of these is the Ramapithecus (Rama's ape), named after the hero of the famous Indian epic the *Ramayana*, just part of the evidence that Asia did play a role in human evolution.

We are on firmer ground in the story of human origin in the stage known as Homo erectus because of the finds summarized under the term Peking man. These were large-headed, upright human forms who clustered in caves and rock shelters, hunted and gathered intensively in the Middle Pleistocene temperate climate of North China, used fire in hearths, and had close relatives in Java. The tools of Homo erectus are often described as chopper-chopping tools, which are basically sizable stone pebbles flaked to produce cutting or chopping edges. These tools are widespread in eastern and southern Asia and have been found along the river terraces of Southeast Asia. In Burma, the material fre-

A fossil-hunting party returns loaded with fossils from a three-day trip along the workings of Dragon Bone Ridge. The Chinese believed fossils were dragon bones and had great curative properties when powdered and eaten; Chinese pharmacists often led museum scientists to rich fossil quarries. In this way Peking man was discovered. (W. Granger, 1922–23)

quently used is petrified wood, but the characteristic tool is identical to those of China. In Indo-Pakistan, they also occur as part of the so-called Soan industry, but here they are mixed with the famous hand axes known in the west from England to Kenya, from France to as far south as Madras on the subcontinent. For this reason many prehistorians believe that the two industries of east and west were made by morphically similar hominids—that is, Homo erectus. As such, the Homo erectus stage represents early man's widest distribution before the appearance of essentially modern man.

In the early 1920s, the discovery of Peking man in the quarried limestone and conglomerate hill known as Chou-k'ou-tien, some thirty miles west of Peking, created a sensation for its time. It seemed to prove the Mother Asia thesis on the one hand, and on the other it was the first time that fossil men of Homo erectus character were actually found together with their tools, hearths, and remnants of food. (Some forty individuals were identified at the site.) Referred to as Sinanthropus, man of China, and in the reconstructions shown as a rather bestial-appearing, heavy-browed, hirsute, and stooped individual, Peking man beautifully fitted the public image of an ape man. The term "missing link" was also commonly used in placing Peking man in his evolutionary place. This was further explained by the Dutch paleontologist G. H. von Koenigswald, who had discovered forms of Java man that revealed similarities to Peking man. Von Koenigswald also found fossil molar teeth in the Chinese stores of Hong Kong and Canton which were not only similar at first examination to those of Peking man but were in some cases three times larger! The concept of giant men set in the context of a "missing link" theory was further enhanced by Franz Weidenreich, a superb human morphologist who painstak-

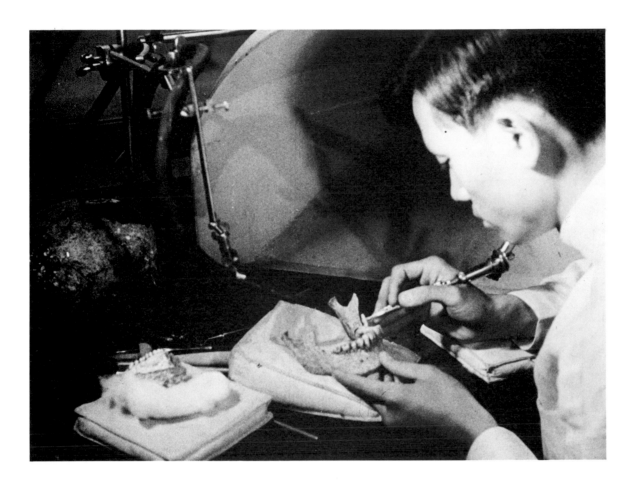

A Chinese assistant to Franz Weidenreich cleans a fossil jaw of Peking man. (c. 1935)

Franz Weidenreich, a German anatomist and anthropologist, examines a skull cap of Peking man. Weidenreich was in charge of the Peking man fossils at the Peking Union Medical College, where he made the definitive study of them in the 1930s. Just before Japan invaded China in 1941, Weidenreich came to the United States and worked at the American Museum of Natural History. After his arrival, he learned that the Peking man fossils had disappeared; they have never been recovered. (c. 1935)

ingly studied Peking man's remains when he published a theoretical account in the Anthropological Papers of the American Museum of Natural History of giant primate forms as possible links in the chain of human evolution.

Today we are aware that Weidenreich's giants or Gigantopithecus are probably an earlier offshoot from the family of which Ramapithecus was a part. Gigantopithecus was a great ape, comparable in size at least with numerous large mammals of the later Tertiary period. Peking man, too, has lost the "missing link" status primarily because more sophisticated ideas of man's evolution preclude the simplistic notion that any one form of fossil "man-ape" is a missing link. All forms of fossil primates are complements to the story of evolution and not links as such.

For this reason as well as the devotion of Franz Weidenreich, the fact that the Peking man remains disappeared during World War II is not as much a loss to science as it otherwise might be, serious enough as it is. Since World War II other remains of Homo erectus have been found in China, some datable as far back as five hundred thousand years, proving the extraordinary time-and-space range of this stage of man's terrestrial existence.

Neanderthal man, a taller, heavier, and larger-brained form of man, must otherwise have appeared somewhat like Peking man, with his chinlessness and striking brow ridges. But culturally it is quite a different matter, because the Neanderthals are, in all but facial appearance, perfectly modern men. They are believed to have existed at the beginning of the Upper Pleistocene, perhaps even as early as 250,000 years ago, and to have died out some 50,000 years ago. Neanderthals are known widely in Western Europe,

Indian Point, Siberia, is the easternmost tip of the Asian continent and is populated by the Asiatic Eskimo, closely related to the North American Eskimo. A popular pastime of both groups is "springing" on a walrus hide. (Waldemar Borgoras, 1901)

48

particularly since the first fossil man identified was found in Germany, followed by a succession of discoveries in France, Belgium, Spain, Italy, England, and Central Europe; it is now known that Neanderthals frequented much of Africa and West Asia. In the 1930s Dorothy Garrod, a British prehistorian, found ten Neanderthals in caves at Mount Carmel near Haifa; Ralph Solecki found seven others in the Shanidar Cave in the Kurdish hills of Iraq; and still others have been discovered in caves in Iran. Most dramatic, however, was the discovery by Russian prehistorians of a Neanderthal child in a cave in the mountains of Teshik Tash in Soviet Central Asia. This child was deliberately wrapped in goatskins at death and then buried near a hearth in the midst of an extensive rock shelter. Particularly revealing was the fact that mountain-goat horns were arranged about the burial as a kind of ritual fence. The mountain-goat is a difficult animal to bag even with a rifle, so the ability of these Neanderthal men of Teshik Tash to capture and kill mountain goats in spite of the limits of their technology is a comment on their hunting prowess, which must have been infinitely skilled. The technology of Neanderthal man is widely referred to as the Mousterian. It is characterized by an industry of tools made out of stone flakes and small flint cores, and includes a varied repertory of stone points, scrapers, knives, choppers, and axes, and also some made of wood, bone, and ivory. This technology stands in striking contrast to the primitive choppers and chopping tools of the previous Homo erectus stage, fine as many of them might be.

Most students of fossil man suspect that the Neanderthals have directly evolved from the Homo erectus stage, to which there appear to be so many resemblances. Something which is not at all clear, but of great interest, when comparing Homo erectus with the Australopithecines, is the evidence of a cultural evolution; there are differences in sophistication and variety between the earlier tool kits of Homo erectus and Neanderthal, and in the deliberate burial of individuals (the child of Teshik Tash), duplicated by finds of deliberate burial of Neanderthals in western Europe. Such burials were not simply a means of disposing of the dead, but showed an apparent formal way of doing so. In Europe, fine tools and ornaments are sometimes found with these burials, suggestive of funerary furniture necessary in afterlife, something that the goat horns of the Teshik Tash burial support. Whatever the significance, it is clear that Neanderthal man gives us evidence for a cognitive development that opens the road to eventual civilization. This needs some explanation.

With the appearance of essentially modern man (Homo sapiens), human evolution appears to have reached a climax of sorts. For certainly no other primate, fossil or living, has achieved the nonorganic, self-perpetuating, adaptive flexibility that modern man has achieved by the development of culture. Culture, as the anthropologist defines it, pertains to the whole behavioral quality of human beings. It is essentially nonorganic in character; that is, it is not passed on through the genes but rather by imitation, precept, and education. It is, of course, strongly related to organic behavioral activity, which appears to be generically motivational to culture as a whole. Anthropologists have considerable difficulty in separating organic from cultural behavior in certain spheres of human activity.

What is important is that because man has created culture, he has achieved the greatest natural adaptability of any organism on earth. The Eskimo of the Siberian Arctic and the Arab of the Arabian desert represent adaptation to two climatic extremes. They symbolize this extraordinary human capability to exist on the earth's surface in almost all ecological niches. This is nowhere so clear as it is in Asia, where climatic extremes and a staggering variety of environments can be found, from the uplands of Tibet, where pastoralists spend much of their lives at elevations above twelve thousand feet, to the Baluch of Kachhi, where the mean annual temperature ranges above 90 degrees Fahrenheit. Clearly the clothing, types of shelter, subsistence habits, social customs, and ideologies of these people have evolved to make possible their effective survival in the ecological situation in which they find themselves. A continent such as Asia, with its great variety of environmental kinds, will have a great variety of cultures. This is, of course, in the strictest sense the mark of modern man's success in being selected out to survive wherever he goes.

Whereas the Australopithecines seemed to be confined to the Old World's warm, even tropical, zones of the south, just as are most primates, Homo erectus not only lived in warm regions, but the Peking man evidence indicates that he also invaded more temperate zones. Neanderthal man went even farther, if the Teshik Tash child of the mountains of Central Asia is any indication. But modern man spreads the world over; he is the universal primate on the face of the earth. He seems to have shown his adaptation by developing varieties of himself that we refer to as races.

Race, then, is a variety of modern man that appears to have occurred as a consequence of adaptation to ecological situations. The Mongoloid races of northern and eastern Asia apparently represent an adaptation to a very cold climate. Indeed, some physical anthropologists suspect that such things as the epicanthic fold around the eyes, the broad Mongoloid face with underlying layers of fat, and the relative hairlessness of the face are an adaptive response to an extremely cold climate such as must have existed during the last glaciation of the Ice Age, or Upper Pleistocene. Narrow eye apertures, insulated cheeks, and lack of hair around the mouth where otherwise the breath's moisture would collect and freeze are advantageous anatomical features in this environment. A recent study of European and Eskimo reactions to cold demonstrates how pervasive climatic conditions are in their effect on organic man. The arms of Europeans and Eskimos were immersed in ice water. At first both reacted similarly in that their limbs felt cold, but as time went on the Europeans' blood pressure, which went up initially, fell, and the flow of blood through the blood vessels was increasingly restricted because of their constriction. Thus the Europeans not only lost the dexterity of their fingers and hands but also their tolerance of the cold. In the Eskimos, almost precisely the reverse happened.

The capability of the Sherpa of Nepal to breathe normally at far higher altitudes than Europeans, and of the bedouin of Jordan to live in heat impossible for other people to bear for long are other demonstrations of this remarkable physiological capability of modern man to adapt to the environmental conditions in which he finds himself. This certainly was a significant factor in the development of the races of modern man and of their cultures.

Realizing this marvelous characteristic of human adaptability, one can begin to understand why civilization came into being and why civilization took different forms in its

The Maritime Koryak lived primarily by fishing and hunting sea mammals on the shores of the Sea of Okhotsk. The men hunted; sometimes girls such as this one tended the lines at ice holes. They suffered greatly when American whaling ships drove away the walrus. (Waldemar Jochelson, 1900)

The annual trading fairs allowed Siberian peoples to meet and barter the scarce goods required for survival in their harsh land. The fairs were also a prime collecting ground for museum anthropologists; Borgoras visited this fair at Yarpol in 1901, but found that a devastating measles epidemic and starvation caused by American whaling and fishing had greatly reduced attendance. (Waldemar Borgoras, 1901)

evolution. This is not to say that there is a direct line between any particular variety of man and particular civilization, but rather to point out that civilization may very well be the consequence of environmental and cultural challenges to which modern man had to respond to survive. This would be perfectly in keeping with man's natural adaptive capability, one that made survival possible through the Pleistocene and into the modern state of the physical earth.

The first civilization known to man appeared in Asia and consequently influenced, in one way or another, the development of other civilizations. However, prior to the first appearance, there must have been active some adaptive challenge to modern man for which civilization was a special response. What was that challenge?

To understand the answer it is necessary to view man not in the context of simple environmental challenge but rather one of physiological response formula. We are becoming aware that the human mind, with its unmatched capability of retaining and storing impressions gained through experience and then using what is learned to act in a variety of situations, some of them of enormous complexity, has to be understood if we are to comprehend human history. The Nirvana of the Buddhists, the Tao of the followers of Lao Tzu, and the kami of the Shintoists are conceptions of such abstractness that they are on a par with the higher mathematics of the savants of Western civilization. Are these abstractions the response to specific kinds of challenges similar in function to the rise of blood pressure of the Eskimo, or the straw hut of the Semai of Malaysia to the jungle? Do they represent a survival mechanism?

It is apparent that all cultures have their reason to be. What cultures do, what form they take, and how they survive is the result of how well the culture functions for the human beings who have created it. It then follows that the myriad cultures of traditional Asia are at best the effective responses of the particular societies to the circumstances in which they have found themselves. These circumstances include not only adaptation to given ecological situations but also cumulative responses to traditional histories in which cultural adaptation to indigenously motivated change, as well as integration with outside alien influences, has taken place. In other words, that which has worked for a people in time and space characterizes its form. At the same time, some cultures change rapidly so that it is sometimes hard to define them from one century (or even generation) to the next; others are conservative and their traditions are recognizable over the millennia. All this change, slow or rapid, demonstrates adaptation just as does the original adjustment to the local geography.

If we examine the differences among these cultures, we discover not only differences in dress, house type, toys, marriage customs, eating habits, and the like, but often strikingly different views and understandings of the world as a whole. The Ainu of Japan, the aboriginal people of the major Japanese islands, had successfully clung to their way of life until they were expelled or assimilated. The Japanese on the other hand were enormously influenced by Chinese culture, accepting the writing system, Buddhism, and much of the esthetic and philosophical ideas along with the technology of that land. Nothing represents so clearly Japanese willingness to integrate inventions and ideas from other cultures as does the enormous Westernization of the country since 1860. This willingness has its fruits in Japan's present status as the most industrialized nation of the world.

What has made the Ainu a conservative culture and the Japanese culture so apparently dynamically nonconservative? Clearly there is a relationship between the historical circumstances of a given culture and its eventual world view. One group of Japanese ancestors came to Japan as a people basically Central Asian in character; to function in the Japanese land they had to emphasize agriculture, for Japan is a land of mountains and hardly conducive to a life of pastoralism. The resulting culture combined village farming with a social and political organization based on clans and chiefdoms. This combination was completely successful, except in regard to their world view. The concept the Japanese had of themselves and the world included a sense of coming from somewhere else, which in their creation myth was literally a descent from the realm of the Sun Goddess (one of the reasons for the appellation "Land of the Rising Sun"). Through the centuries, the Japanese created an elite ideal that was impossible to live up to, for it not only made Japanese believe that they were superior to foreigners but it also made them uncomfortable with mere status quo, no matter how successful it might be. Japanese history is a story of the rise and fall of given political powers as well as cultural institutions in many areas of life—this in spite of the inherent economic stability given by intensive and remunerative agricultural and fishing activity. The Ainu, on the other hand, have a basic dependence on hunting and gathering that appears to be an often precarious situation; but it is not, because there is an abundance of game and plants, and because Ainu methods of seeking their subsistence are expert and efficient.

The Ainu see their world as a unity of deities, demons, spirits, and human beings; to them, the supernatural world is simply Ainu life enlarged to a scale beyond the capacities of normal men and women. Man and deity interrelate through ritual acts, shamanism, taboo, and sacrifice. This interrelationship is unquestioned. There is no science beyond the needs of daily life, nor motivation to speculate on ultimate meanings. Myth, legend,

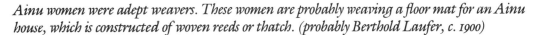

Ainu women were adept weavers. These women are probably weaving a floor mat for an Ainu house, which is constructed of woven reeds or thatch. (probably Berthold Laufer, c. 1900)

The Ainu are sometimes referred to as the "hairy Ainu" because of their abundant body hair, which sets them apart from other Asian groups. This Ainu man sits before his tea-ceremony bowl and mustache stick. The stick is used by the Ainu to keep the mustache out of tea and sake. The carved stick is also used as a libation wand, believed to carry prayers properly to the spirits. (probably Berthold Laufer, c. 1900)

The Ainu of Japan were easily recognizable by the lip tattoo of the women and the heavy beard of the men—both signs of Ainu adulthood. The origins of the Ainu have been a mystery to anthropologists; physically, culturally, and linguistically they are like no other East Asian group. In addition to the unusually heavy beards of the men, many Ainu have distinctly Caucasian features and some have blue eyes. Some anthropologists speculate that they may be an ancient group of Caucasians who migrated across Siberia and were the first settlers of the Japanese and eastern Siberian islands. The ethnic Japanese were later invaders from the mainland who displaced the Ainu, gradually pushing them farther north. The twentieth century has seen the end of this ethnic group and their way of life; perhaps only one hundred full-blooded Ainu remain, and the language is no longer spoken except in prayer and song. (probably Berthold Laufer, c. 1900)

Tibetan Buddhism had a substantial following among Tibetans in northern China. Here a group of Chinese gather at the Lama Temple (Yung Ho Kung) in Peking to watch a Tibetan dance performed by monks. (before 1912)

and folklore are present in both Ainu and Japanese culture, but the characters of Ainu story are drawn directly and largely from nature: fire, bears, foxes, seals, fish, trees. The Japanese emphasize human beings—even the gods are human in aspect. Ainu deities act as their manifestations act, but Japanese spirits often behave like men, even assuming the irrational aspects of Homo sapiens.

Knowing that such differences occur between cultures existing even in the same region, we can understand what must have been the situation toward the close of the Ice Age. Modern man by this time had spread to the limits of the Old World wherever there was ice-free land and where hunting and gathering was productive. People established themselves in given areas largely by living in seasonal camps that were chosen according to where the greatest concentration of game and edible plants was to be found. At Dolní Věstonice in southern Slovakia, for example, hunters of young mammoths built a winter camp by a stream on a hillside above a large river valley. Some twenty-five thousand years ago central Europe was in the lee of the northern ice sheets of the last great glaciation. The temperatures through nine months of the year must have ranged well below zero Fahrenheit. The hills were perpetually snow-covered, but in the sheltered valleys coniferous trees, northern reeds, bushes, and grasses survived. Concentrated here in the height of the winter were herds of mammoths, the basic foodstuff of the hunters, who used not only the meat but the large bones, which were made into a wall around their camp. Their tool kit had at least three times the repertory of Neanderthal man's Mousterian assemblages. Based on the flint blade, a narrow object delicately removed from a prepared flint core, their tools included a variety of knives, scrapers, engravers, and points, which can be likened to a dentist's shelves of utensils made for almost every contingency. Among these objects are delicate flint saws with sharp teeth which could be hafted into wooden holders and used to saw or sickle as the case may be. These saws are symptomatic of the keen interest Upper Pleistocene man had in plant life as a source of food and for other uses. This, of course, was nothing new in the life of prehistoric man, for it is well known from modern ethnographic parallels that among hunters and gatherers the whole landscape furnished the natural resources for their life, not just a part of it. To do this a fundamental knowledge of the life cycle of plants and animals was required and was basic to the origin of civilization.

Outside the immediate camp of the Dolní Věstonice mammoth hunters and partially dug into the side of the hill was a hut in which hundreds of fragments of animal figurines were found near a fire pit. Obviously these figurines had been baked by the fire, but it appears that some effort had been made to regulate the heat by blowing through clay tubes. In other words, fire was not simply a source of warmth, cookery, light, and safety, but a necessary resource in the rather complex chore of changing river clay into a durable figurine. Again we are witness to the sophistication of prehistoric man's awareness of the utility of material things.

Near to the hut was found the grave of a female whose face was distorted on the left

(text continued on page 69)

The old city of Samarkand, seen here in ruins, is one of the oldest cities in Central Asia. It was captured by Alexander the Great in 329 B.C., and again captured and destroyed by Genghis Khan in A.D. 1220. At the end of the fourteenth and beginning of the fifteenth centuries, Tamerlane (Timur) made it the capital of his empire, and it became an important economic and cultural center. It is located in Uzbekistan, today a part of the Soviet Union. (Epstein, recent)

56

The best-known example of an early human ancestor from Asia is Peking man from the cave of Chou-k'ou-tien, near Peking. These hominids, assigned to the species Homo erectus, *lived about half a million years ago. The cast shown here is of a reconstruction of a male skull made by Dr. Franz Weidenreich. None of the original specimens (now lost) is this complete.*

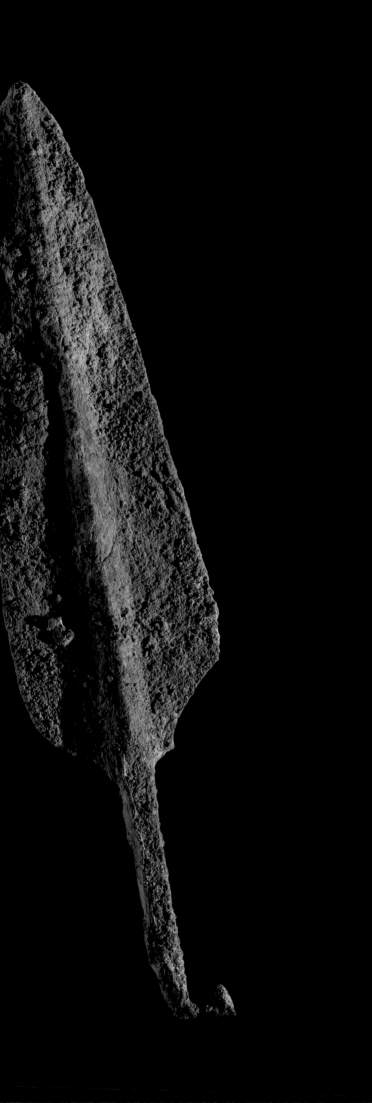

Village farming, which spread to the Iranian plateau around 6500 B.C., allowed for social stability and leisure time, both of which may have led to the smelting of copper. This spearpoint excavated at Tepe Hissar, Damghan, Iran, may date from about 2000 B.C. Height: 20 inches

OPPOSITE:

This Bronze Age goblet (c. 3000 B.C.) was excavated at Tepe Hissar, Damghan, Iran, an important Bronze Age site. The geometric design is typical of Bronze Age pottery and can be found in a large area encompassing the Iranian plateau and parts of Central Asia. Height: 6 inches

This bronze forepart of a bull with its legs folded under is reminiscent of Achaemenid Persia. Height: 2½ inches

OPPOSITE:

From about 2400 to 1800 B.C. the Indus Valley civilization flourished from Pakistan to a large area in India stretching a thousand miles from Delhi in the north to the Narbada River in the south. The author excavated this clay figurine, which stands scarcely three inches tall, in Pakistan. It is one of the earliest examples of sculpture from the Indian subcontinent; the delicacy of the figure, especially in the strands of knotted hair descending over the shoulders, reveals great artistic sensitivity. The meaning of the figure is unknown.

In the ancient Near East, 3000 B.C. to 2000 B.C., a bull such as this bronze was the vehicle of the weather god. Its horns are divine symbols and appear on the caps of the gods and on shrines and altars. Height: 4¹/₂ inches

OPPOSITE:

This carved and painted wooden mask-hanging from Sri Lanka was placed on a wall during a ceremony for curing an illness. The small masks on it represent devils associated with disease. Full-scale masks of these kinds were used in the dance ceremony itself. Height: 43 inches

OPPOSITE:

Ferocious devil posts were placed along the roads leading into a Korean village to protect it from wandering evil spirits. Height: (left) 69½ inches; (right) 70 inches

The huti *is a stringed instrument played with a horsetail bow, much like a violin. This instrument was crafted by Pathans, who live in the rugged mountains of the Khyber Pass area. Height: 24 inches*

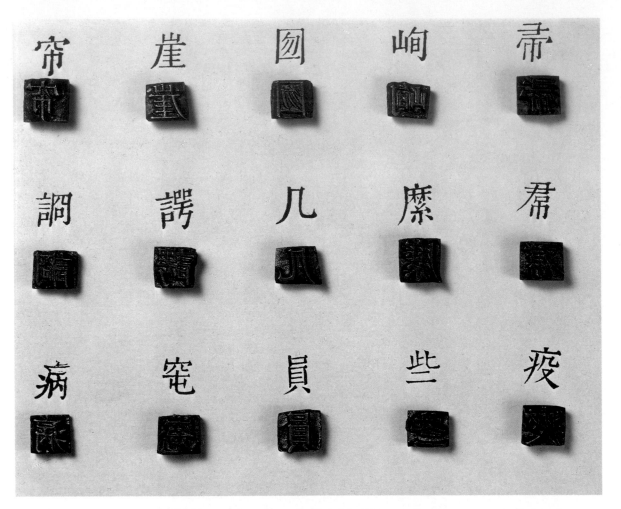

Movable metal type was developed in Korea at least two centuries before the Gutenberg Bible was printed in 1440, and printing with wood blocks was in use as early as the eighth century. One example of wood-block printing that was recently found in Korea dates from A.D. 751 and is the oldest printed text in the world. The bronze type shown here is believed to be from the extremely rare Kyemi type font of 1403. The characters are Chinese since all official documents were written in that language. However, one of the achievements of the Korean civilization was the Korean alphabet invented by King Sejong in the early fifteenth century. It was used for unofficial purposes, particularly by women. Average height of type: 1/2 inch

OPPOSITE:

The eclectic influences in Central Asian crafts can be seen in this assortment of hats (kolas) made by the Uzbeks and other tribal groups. Invasion and trade brought Central Asians in contact with many other areas; their crafts, especially weaving and metalwork, show these varied influences. Average dimension: 8 inches

Kashgar is located in Singkiang in an oasis on the ancient highway running through Central Asia. Although it no longer is a place of hustling trade, the bazaar remains. (J. L. Clark, c. 1920s)

(text continued from page 56)

side. An ivory carving of a human face with the same distortion was recovered from the living camp. The image was duplicated by an ivory buttonlike object found also in the camp. The body was contracted and lay under two mammoth scapulae; near her hand was the remains of an arctic fox, by her head was a flint point, and she was covered with red-ocher stains. The general conclusion is that this strange woman lived in the hut outside the camp, and because of her unusual appearance and, presumably, behavior she had a role as a shamaness—that is, was regarded as one who could contact the supernatural, probably by going into a trance and by so doing persuade or coerce the supernatural to the benefit of the living. The special treatment demonstrated in her burial shows a concern by the living for the dead, probably in fear of supernatural retaliation for neglect of suitable rites.

The well-known cave paintings and other art forms of France and Spain, and the "mother goddesses" of central and eastern Europe, all seem to attest to beliefs of one

In this sixteenth-century Nepalese brass image showing the miraculous birth of Buddha, the infant springs from the right side of his mother, Queen Maya, as she supports herself by holding on to a tree limb. This pose reflects the standard depiction of the Indian Yakshi, *the ancient female nature force that predates Buddhism. Height: 52½ inches*

69

A Reindeer Koryak boy demonstrates his toy bow and arrow. The Reindeer Koryak is an aboriginal group living in Siberia and in the past was dependent on large herds of reindeer for travel, food, and clothing. (Waldemar Jochelson, 1900)

kind or another, including the efficacy of magic. As Marschak has shown recently, Upper Pleistocene man also had a cognitive capability in that he used simple notation to record the passing of the days of the lunar month and of the months themselves.

In all, the end of the Ice Age was witness to modern man's effective adaptation to a myriad of ecological circumstances. We can assume that most of the cultures existing were, like the Ainu of Japan, relatively stable in their representation of a unity of man in nature. For indeed, man in those days, as among aboriginal people of recent times, felt himself to be as much a part of nature as stars, reeds, animals, and stones. To nature he owed a familial obligation—personal, reciprocal, and necessary. Nature was not to be exploited at will. What was used must be accounted for by ritual acknowledgement or secular conservation.

The prehistorian reviewing the cultural manifestations on the Eurasian and African continents of postglacial times lists people in Europe dependent on reindeer; people on the Caspian Sea using seals and voles as the basis of their diet; people in North Africa hunting African parkland fauna; and people in the Levant and into the hills of the Near East hunting gazelle, deer, wild goats, and sheep. New instrumentation in archeology now has given prehistorians evidence for plants also: hazelnuts in Europe; wild cereals in the Near East; legumes everywhere. Where there had been a degree of uniformity in subsistence pursuits by people of the late stages of the Ice Age, now, in post-Ice Age times, there was increasing diversity in Europe at least. As the essentially modern climate came into being there were more viable ecological niches to fit within.

Throughout the Upper Pleistocene, European cultures were increasingly elaborating so that by 12,000 B.C. the prehistoric men of western Europe appeared to have achieved a cultural climax that permitted the unity of several thousand people in one place and the cohesiveness economically, socially, politically, and ideologically to keep them functioning as large units, perhaps tribes, for a considerable period of time. Whenever large numbers of people were together, the exchanged ideas spread widely to all individuals, sometimes motivating new ideas and thus innovations. Since these people were consummate observers of the landscape, they knew the whole spectrum of its benefits and adversities. They had an excellent, efficient, and reliable technology; social cohesion; notational sophistication; and an ideological awareness capable of dealing with the exigencies of their daily life.

It was not in Europe that civilization had its origins but in the Asian Near East. It was also there that the first agriculture and animal domestication took place. There was no indication anywhere in Asia of the cultural elaboration achieved in Europe, or of the perception evidenced by the cultures of Late Pleistocene Europe. Most of Asia, except the Near East, appears to have been almost a full step behind. In northern and Central Asia along the Siberian margin, Mousterian-like industries were still the basic tool resources of the hunters and gatherers living there. In Southeast Asia, China, and Japan, the Upper Paleolithic, as the blade tool assemblages known in Europe are generally labeled, was almost entirely absent. In some cases chopper-chopping tools were still being used in modified form. Only recently something of an Upper Paleolithic has been defined for India. But nowhere in Asia was there quite the elaborate technology, or the evidence for the kind of cognitive development as shown by cave paintings, sculptures, and size of settlements, as in Europe. Clearly, then, the origin of civilization was not the direct consequence of the cultural sophistication that was the climax of European prehistory.

During the past three decades R. J. Braidwood of the Oriental Institute of the University of Chicago conducted a series of strategically placed archeological studies in the Near East. Braidwood was looking for the prehistoric roots of man's first civilization, the Sumerian. That civilization depended for its subsistence basis, as did its slightly later

The Kalmucks are a small group descended from the last Mongol invaders to enter Russia, and live in the arid Kalmyk Steppe of southern Russia. Like most Mongol groups, they depend on felt for covering their yurts, or dwellings, and for a variety of other uses. These women are making felt in the traditional manner by laying clean wool out on a large cloth; they will later soak the wool in whey and lay another cloth over it. The two cloths are tightly rolled on a long pole and bound, and the cylinder is rolled behind a horse. The compressed sheet of wool felt is dried in the sun, and its edges are sewn to prevent fraying. (J. L. Clark, c. 1920s)

The nomads of Tibet made boats from the skins of the yak, a hirsute animal resembling a bison. These frail skin coracles, when used with care, could carry up to three people and two hundred pounds of cargo. They are propelled by a man who kneels in the bow and paddles. Yaks have long been domesticated by the Tibetans, who also weave yak hair into a thick cloth for tents, robes, and blankets, and depend on the yak as a beast of burden.

counterpart in Egypt, on the cultivation of wheat and barley, the energies of domesticated cattle and onagers, and the flesh and hair of goats and sheep. Though something was known in the 1930s of the pre-Sumerian cultural assemblages, there was no clear evidence for either the origin of civilized institutions or of agriculture and animal domestication. However, deep digging at sites in southern Mesopotamia and Assyria revealed village cultures in a kind of sequence, ranging from small settlements with little differentiation among the structures and an emphasis on essentially cottage industries of pottery, weaving, and simple metallurgy to large settlements grouped around public buildings, usually a temple on a mound, with standardized industries, including a complex metallurgy, a system of notation, and the beginnings of a system of writing. In addition, there was evidence of the development of plow agriculture, the use of the wheel in several ways, and the use of irrigation. Though many of the surveys were incomplete, they demonstrated that the different periods, in which the sequence described above occurred, existed throughout the Near East generally. Indeed, there was some evidence that trade took place between many of the settlements.

Braidwood, well aware of this sequence, was concerned to define its origins, for throughout Mesopotamia the cultivation of the cereal grains and the use of domesticated sheep and goats were a constant theme. Clearly that fact marked the Near Eastern development, particularly the Mesopotamian, and set it off from the European. There was, of course, a time factor: the Mesopotamian sequence, as then known, dated from about 6000 B.C. to 3500 B.C., or, in its beginnings, some six thousand or more years after the

European climax. In temporal terms, let alone spatial, the European contribution to the sequence in the Near East appears to be minimal. One major and crucial difference between the European and the Near Eastern situation was economic; one depended on hunting and gathering, the other on plant and animal domestication. Clearly, then, the start of the Near Eastern sequence leading to civilization was the origin of domestication itself. But where was one to look for that origin?

Older theories stated that when the ice retreated at the end of the Pleistocene, the earth's climatic zone belts, which had been compressed against the tropical equator by the Arctic zone's shift southward, now moved north and brought significant changes to the climate of any given region. Previously, North Africa and the Near East had enjoyed the benefits of substantial rainfall when the temperate zone was the climatic doctrine of those regions; in consequence, park and forest lands, teeming with game and edible plants, were a kind of Eden where man in his innocence could obtain his subsistence at ease. Now began the inexorable drying up that led to the modern deserts which characterize North Africa and the Near East today. Only the great river systems, whose drainage areas included perennial sources of moisture, and the mountains could sustain life for man, beast, and plant in the growing aridity. As a consequence, the whole biota migrated into those moist valleys where men, now more intimately thrown together, perceived the values inherent in domestication. Thus began the cultural evolution leading to the civilizations that were situated in the very valleys where domestication had begun.

The problem was that the first animals and plants domesticated were *not* indigenous to the great river valleys, nor was there any indication that rainfall had slackened in the time period in which it was supposed to have occurred. The first domesticates in their feral state were all highland inhabitants. If the evidence for early domestication existed, it had to be found in what Robert J. Braidwood called the hilly flanks of the Fertile Crescent. The Fertile Crescent, a term coined by the Egyptologist James Henry Breasted, meant the river valleys and fertile areas that extended in a great crescent from the Nile Valley through the Levant and down the Tigris and Euphrates river valleys to the Arabo-Persian Gulf. The hilly flanks, largely on the Mesopotamian side, meant the mountains and foothills above the crescent. While working in these hills Braidwood and his successors found not only wild forms of wheat and barley but archeological sites that showed a transition of sorts between hunting-gathering and life based on primary village farming.

It has been shown that a family in a few weeks' time could gather enough wild wheat to provide subsistence for an entire year. Though wheat kernels are digestible after the husk is removed, they are much more so when cooked as a kind of popcorn, or ground into flour mixed with water and baked into bread. This mixing with water can in time bring about fermentation and thus a crude beer. But the gathering of wild wheat is not like picking blueberries for it involves a clear sense of a process to be undertaken. It is no coincidence that these early sites revealed that the original inhabitants had grinding stones, mortars and pestles, and containers ostensibly to hold the flour that was the product of the pounding and grinding process. Nothing proves so much the sophistication of the human mind as the capability to conceive of a final product before it is made and then, by a sequence of activity, bring the imagined into reality. In effect, the more steps necessary to make an idea a reality, the greater the complexity of thought. But these steps can only be arrived at initially by experimentation, by the step-by-step procedures of trial and error, leading to eventual success.

Since the achievement of the domestication process is a landmark in man's evolution, Braidwood and his team of experts in geology, mammalogy, botany, and archeology were recovering evidence of enormous importance. For one can ask the question why and how did man abandon the hunting-gathering way of life which had worked so well for the species for hundreds of thousands of years? The answer may lie in the fact that man has the ability to remember experience in nature and to pass that experience along so that succeeding generations need not replicate it. Knowledge carried by man's culture through time is cumulative. In general, man's cognitive evolution results in citizens of later cultures knowing more than those earlier in time. The evolution is not always clear, for often mankind dreams of golden ages in the past. But in terms of sheer growth of knowledge there is no question that we know more today about the world than the Europeans of the eighteenth century, and they in turn more than those of the sixteenth century, and so on backward in time. Our knowledge rooted in the past has accumulated constantly, an obvious fact that is axiomatic to an understanding of the genesis of human invention. In technology at least, men profit by one another's mistakes until the final product can be made without error.

As described previously, man had a consummate knowledge of the life cycles of the plants and animals of the ecological niches that he was exploiting. Among these niches, according to the Braidwood scheme, are the ones possessing potentially domesticable plants and animals. Asia has a number of such places: Southeast Asia—rice, silk worm, water buffalo; India—rice, cotton, water buffalo, humped cattle; the Near East—wheat, barley, goat, sheep, cattle, horse; China—millet, rape, pig. Certain regions have single forms that become domesticated later such as the camel of Central Asia, the yak of Tibet, and the reindeer of Siberia, but Braidwood argues that it is a constellation of potential domesticates that marks what he calls nuclear areas—that is, areas where domestication becomes a prime basis for subsistence.

The hilly flank zone above the Fertile Crescent is such a nuclear area. Some ten thousand years before the birth of Christ men were living there in intimate contact with plants and animals which by habit, nutritional value, and number were particularly important to man. The Natufians of Palestine, who lived in caves on the slopes of Mount Carmel, and the inhabitants of sites such as Karim Shahir in the Kurdish hills of Iraq were among those living in what Braidwood calls a stage of incipience.

Domestication means in effect the ability of man to manipulate the life cycle of an organism for man's benefit. Braidwood's sites of incipience do not show such an occurrence, but the presence of sickle blades and grinding stones indicates that the wild forms of plant life were being used. This is not unexpected since the whole spectrum of plant life was tapped by prehistoric man. But now *certain* species were being utilized more than others, including the wild ancestors of domesticated wheats and barleys. The next sites of the Braidwood scheme are largely found in the hilly flanks of the foothill country. Here evidence established village life which, while still having a degree of dependence on hunting and gathering, emphasized the herding of goats and the cultivation of wheat and barley.

It was a great surprise to many prehistorians, who had expected these early farming villages to be rather primitive clusters of houses with small undifferentiated populations, to discover that there were also sites such as Tell es-Sultan at Jericho, which was a walled town with several thousand inhabitants. The walls were of stone and included a tower some forty feet high, complete with interior stairway. At Çatal Hüyük on the Konya plain of south-central Anatolia, a community existed with a population of more than two thousand who were living in doorless houses placed wall-to-wall and with an entrance through a hole in the roof. Within were elaborate rooms dominated by benches along the walls; frequently the walls were plastered and painted with scenes of hunting ritual, fine animal representations, and geometric and floral designs, the last in patterns suggestive of wall hangings like the kilim of modern Turkey. Çatal Hüyük also gave evidence that women were engaged in agriculture while men continued to hunt, a sexual division of labor which had its symbolism in the placement of female figurines in or near grain bins. The theme of agriculture, birth, and women is a very old one and is manifested in a large number of Asian cultures. Indeed, it is a prominent theme the world over. What is important at Çatal Hüyük is that a symbolism interrelating agriculture, human birth, women, and deity argues for a complexity of thought of considerable sophistication. The so-called Venus figurines, found in Upper Paleolithic Europe at places such as Dolní Věstonice, are so generalized in their indication of fertility or femaleness that they are rather simplistic statements of that fact. That is not the case with the Çatal Hüyük figurines, for clearly agriculture with its sequence of seed to harvest to consumption was regarded as similar to copulation-pregnancy-birth, and therefore women were the obvious custodians of agricultural activity. There is evidence that the dibble stick was used to break the ground, something women could do easily.

The Sinhalese form the largest population (about 70 percent) of the island of Sri Lanka and are primarily Buddhist. This family wears the traditional Sinhalese dress of a length of cloth tucked around the waist and reaching to the ankles, above which the men wear coats or shirts and the women blouses. (Lee Boltin, 1955)

Much later in prehistory, the advent of the plow, which required great strength to maneuver, brought men into agriculture and changed the symbolism.

These sites date around 6500 B.C. or somewhat earlier, and they represent complicated political and social organization necessary to direct the fortunes of many people living together. Direction obviously was needed to organize the group for harvest, large-scale hunting, and mutual protection. There is evidence at Çatal Hüyük of shrines containing clay and plaster images of bulls and other creatures; some areas are elaborate enough to indicate temples. At Jericho, there is, of course, the great stone tower. Thus both sites and their structures show group participation either in building or in the functions for which the buildings were made.

Trade in shells, wood, obsidian, and other nonindigenous materials existed. Clearly, in a large group some regulation of equivalences in exchange was required. There is no sign, however, of any class divisions based on wealth, though it is clear that specialization in some occupations—weaving, stonework, herding, hunting, farming, and administration—was necessary.

Pottery made its appearance about this time apparently as a more substantial substitute for wooden vessels. Wooden prototypes for pottery vessels have been found at Çatal Hüyük. The various steps necessary to make a pot in clay—obtaining the raw material, treating it, adding some kind of temper, mixing with water, creating the vessel, decorating, and firing—were not simple. Again we see man's growing awareness in prehistoric times of more and more complex processes by which raw materials were converted into functional artifacts. Even at this stage men were using native copper for ornaments, and there is growing evidence for the beginning of smelting.

These Siberians are dressed in typical Manchu clothing, but they could be Manchu, Siberian Tungus, or Mongolian—three related groups. Like many Asian groups, the Manchu (whose language some linguists believe is more closely related to Finnish and Hungarian than Chinese) borrowed from and contributed to Chinese culture during their 250-year rule of that country. (Waldemar Borgoras, 1900)

The domestication of goats and sheep, possibly as a consequence of pet-keeping, as well as the dependencies by flocks on man, had two consequences. First, these browsers and grazers had to be controlled if the growing grain was to survive. Thus the flocks were obviously kept apart from the fields, even though some were tethered in the settlement proper. The flocks were supplements to the field produce which at this time, as a consequence of further experiments in cultivation, included the vetches, peas, beans, and possibly the pomegranate, besides wheat and barley. The second consequence was the appearance of groups who depended *solely* on flocks. These people must have had to shift seasonally to obtain the necessary grass for their flocks. Probably they had symbiotic relationships with the settled villages in which the produce of the flocks was exchanged for the produce of the fields. We have little knowledge of these people because they have left little archeological trace. But in view of the broad economic division in Asia in later times between village farming with local pastoralism and the pastoral nomad with his camp, there is little doubt that domestication in prehistoric times had these two basic emphases. This division plays a considerable role in the Asian ethos.

The next stage in the development toward civilization in Mesopotamia was apparently the movement of village farming out of uplands into lower regions. This meant, of course, that village farmers were moving plant and animal life indigenous to one environment into another. Clearly, in the case of plants they were using artificial selection to do so, choosing plants with survival value in lower regions and breeding to that value. Moving from the rolling plains of Assyria where rainfall made the soil moist, early farmers steadily shifted south-eastward past the plains around modern Baghdad into the alluvial plain of Shinar, which is located between the Tigris and Euphrates rivers. This plain, rich in soil, is subject to flooding much as the Nile River, and these floods maintain the soil fertility by soil replacement. The surrounding area is desert, and the climate is hot and arid. A degree of vigilance was necessary to support any sizable population, for unless one lived close to the rivers, tapping the water as needed, water had to be brought to fields away from the rivers.

Initially the farmers who settled in Shinar apparently did stay close to the rivers, which in this flat, open region tend to meander, providing loops of moist, fertile soil and flood-plain braiding. These early farmers were hardly primitive village dwellers, for the evidence is that they had a sophisticated tool kit well suited for farming; made handsome painted pottery; cultivated dates in addition to the large spectrum of cultivated food plants; had cattle, sheep, and goats; and lived in sizable, mud-brick settlements, some of which were centered around temples set on artificial mounds. They had commercial and possibly kin ties in surrounding regions northwest and southeast of Shinar. They used square-rigged riverboats; knew the use of the seal as a marker of property; and made clay figurines suggestive of the old fertility cults like those postulated for Çatal Hüyük.

Irrigation, possibly to extend the flood plain initially but more and more to insure perennial water to settlements that grew away from the main rivers, made its appearance somewhere in this development of the plain. It seems certain that the population on the plain of Shinar increased owing to the great productivity of the soil and the accumulation of surpluses, making the region especially attractive. Here, then, was the protogenesis of civilization: augmenting populations, public projects, a stable and flourishing economy, outside contacts, systems of distribution, the development of specializations such as the coppersmith, weaver, priest, potter, trader, boatman, basket- and reed-worker, and seal-carver.

The growth of symbolism is of great importance. Recently Denise Schmandt has shown that the small clay objects, which are found in some number, particularly in the later stages of cultural developments in Shinar, are actually tokens representing everything from oxen to slave girls. Simply by counting these tokens one could obtain an inventory of possessions or merchandise. As it turns out, these tokens are the predecessors to certain signs in the earliest writing—the proto-Sumerian.

Writing is, of course, symbolism, that is, each sign used in writing either stands for a word or a syllable, or is simply a picture of what is meant. Of all the criteria used to define civilization, writing is probably the most definitive for it argues for a complexity of thought and consequence unparalleled in other forms of culture. The great animal paintings of the Upper Paleolithic of western Europe and the murals at Çatal Hüyük are indeed symbolic, but it seems that they were meant to be taken for themselves only. A picture is a picture of something and meant to be just that. Pictures can be arranged to tell stories, as is demonstrated by the wood carvings of the Koryak of Siberia, which describe hunts by pictures meant to be read in sequence. The Yukaghir wrote letters on bark using stylized, but perfectly understandable, pictures in which men and women are distinguished by the length of their hair, and relationships designated by lines: straight ones for brothers and sisters, wavy ones for married couples or lovers.

For numbers one can make a single stroke for every item, and add items by counting strokes. This is a clumsy method when a great number is desired. If one realizes that there are 30 days in a month, and counts from full moon to full moon, the number 30 could be represented by ◯ the picture of the full moon. Thirty-three is thus ◯ ||| ; supposing one wanted to indicate the third day of the third month, one could write ||| ◯ ||| ; but supposing, instead, one meant 3 thirties plus 3, or 93. Clearly one would have to change ◯ in some way to differentiate month from the number 30. Thus ◯ equals month and ◯ equals the number 30. This change is a fundamental step in the origin of writing for it moves us from looking at ◯ as a full moon to viewing it as a symbol of a number. We have gone from picture to symbol.

The next step is the attachment of sound values to signs, a step that apparently arose out of the idea of combining. Thus ▽ , representing the female vulva in proto-Sumerian, means "girl." ⌂⌂ represents mountains, probably derived from an older picture of mountains like △△△ . By combining ▽⌂⌂, the proto-Sumerians could designate "slave girl" since their slaves came from the mountainous regions to the northeast of Shinar. But there is a limit to what one can do even with these combinations. A rebus system can

be used: eye   can   sea   meaning "I can see." Here the sounds of words are homophonic to one another. The signs are being used for their sounds, not as what they represent as pictures. But there are problems with the rebus because not all words have homophonic equivalents in objects and the meanings can be confused. Take, for example, the two sentences: "The sons raise meat" and "the sun's rays meet." One could write the second sentence like this: sun   rays   meet   and the first sentence   sons   raise   meat. This means that one is drawing a picture for every meaning even though the sounds are the same. Why not classify or determine meaning by sharing the sounds? Thus

○ 大   could mean   ○   *sound* is "sun" but *meaning* is   大   "son." The latter sign determines the meaning of the sound.   ＞＜ 丰   not "rays" but "raise." In time, certain signs were always used for their sounds; after 2000 B.C. alphabets appear where the whole sign system is phonetic.

The sign system of the Sumerians, who are the people who eventually achieved civilization in Mesopotamia on the plain of Shinar, is referred to as cuneiform (Latin, wedge-shape), because the stylus used in writing on the clay tablets, which were the medium in stoneless and paperless Shinar, produced wedge-shaped marks. These wedges outlined the original pictures but through time so turned, involuted, and stylized them that cuneiform writing in large part lost its pictographic genesis. The signs themselves carried a phonetic complement which was more important than what was depicted. In effect, the Sumerians made their writing system more and more efficient by paying greater attention to sound values. They never gave up entirely the classifier technique nor the picture element, but their successors, the Amorite Babylonians, Assyrians, and Achaemenid Persians, did.

About 3400 B.C., the Sumerians, successors in the cultural evolutionary sequence on the plain of Shinar, probably coming from somewhere north of the Iranian plateau, appear to have accelerated cultural developments. By 3200 B.C., the Sumerians had created numerous cities centered around elaborate temples which were situated on high mounds, at critical points on the shores of the great rivers, and also at strategic locations close to enormous irrigation canals. Each city was at the heart of a state. The city and its surrounding landscape had a body of myths and legends confirming its creation as a consequence of divine will and human endeavor. Government was by kings, seconded by nobles, priests, and by the urban citizenry. There were elaborate farming estates and fine city homes for the wealthy. Craftsmen included the goldsmith, the maker of bronze, and the jeweler, and there was more and more demand for foreign luxuries such as silver, lapis lazuli, and ivory. The government had its bureaucracy and included scribes, military officials, and tax collectors. Slaves worked the land, and servants supported the priesthood in the temples. Most Sumerian cities counted more than ten thousand citizens. Urban controls over garbage and sewage disposal, policing streets, fighting fires, regulating the rate of exchange and inheritance problems required the formulation of laws. Laws gained more validity with the extension of a court system complete with judges, bailiffs, and the swearing of witnesses. Law codes were created as a covenant between the gods and the king for the sake of the state. These codes resulted in the great law code of Hammurabi, a non-Sumerian king who followed the demise of Sumerian political power. In all, this earliest civilization had not a little similarity with our modern civilization.

But it was a troubled civilization. The records that have come down to us leave little doubt that warfare between the city states, invading foreigners such as the Elamites of Iran and the Amorites of the Arabian Desert, silting irrigation canals, droughts, storms, and plagues had their role in affecting the Sumerian world view. One of the great epics of Asia tells the story of Gilgamesh, a king of a Sumerian city. He is a superbeing who, with his half-beast friend Enkidu, defeats monsters and offends the gods. In turn, the gods punish him by killing Enkidu. Gilgamesh questions mortality by seeking Utnapishtim, the only human being to achieve immortality by serving the gods at the time of a great flood (with an ark). Utnapishtim cannot help Gilgamesh, who, conscious of his mortality, returns to his duties as king. Not even his strength and power can keep him from eventual death. The Sumerians had schools for learning subjects such as writing. But their theology reiterated that man was created by the gods to labor for them . . . there is no other destiny.

The Sumerians can be characterized as speculative, practical, innovative, perhaps to a degree pessimistic, and they were excellent organizers. Their civilization was dynamic and immensely influential in the time it flourished and for a long while after its demise.

Ancient Sumer stands in contrast to its contemporary, Egypt. The Egyptian civilization in comparison was conservative, largely nonspeculative, isolated, and innovative mostly at the technological level. Hieroglyphic, their logo-syllabic system of writing, changed but little through time. Egyptians seem never to have questioned deity, at least not until later in their history. Their world view can be said to be generally optimistic. But ancient Egypt is not an Asian civilization such as was Sumer. Were the Sumerians the forerunners of Asian civilization elsewhere? Do the early Asian civilizations, and their later manifestations in India and China, emulate the Sumerian in character or are they so unique that comparisons are invalid? This we shall examine in the next chapters.

Western Asia was the seat of the world's earliest animal and plant domestication and of the world's earliest civilization. The link between the two developments is still somewhat tenuous, but it is certain that without agriculture ancient Sumer would not have come into being. But is the trail that leads from the Fertile Crescent's hills down to the plain of Shinar the path man had to take to civilization, or was there a necessary ingredient to be obtained from elsewhere?

Civilizations are linked to change—from their genesis to their demise. A civilized world view involves not only self-satisfaction but a struggle for self-identity, an involvement that characterizes Asian civilization everywhere. Change is the universal rule in the history of Asian civilizations. It is change, then, the search for innovation, that added to the security of subsistence resources and to the challenges of the environment, both physical and cultural, in the plain of Shinar, and which led to the development of Asia's first civilization.

III

THE
NEAR EASTERN
MOSAIC

UNDERSTANDING THE PEOPLE of the Near East is in many ways more difficult for people of the West than any other culture area of Asia. There are two historical reasons for this: Islam and the Turks. The Turks ruled much of southeastern Europe from the early sixteenth century until 1918, and for much of that time they controlled the North African coast and many islands in the Mediterranean. No one familiar with European history, particularly in the sixteenth and seventeenth centuries, can deny the enormous influence the Turks had on Europe. Their control of the eastern Mediterranean made trade with India and other eastern lands difficult, if not impossible. Turkish expansion into central Europe brought Hungary under their control, and Vienna itself was besieged. The most important siege was in 1683, symbolized to this day by the crescent-shaped rolls found in all Viennese coffee shops. It took the combined powers of Poland and the Habsburg monarchy to drive the Turks back; this victory, together with the naval battle of Lepanto (1571) won by John of Austria, represented in European eyes the triumph of the Christian West and of the forces of Good over Evil.

The Turks maintained a ruthless policy during their conquests, killing, raping, burning, and carrying into slavery their captives. It was a deliberate policy to cow those they had conquered. The fact that polygamy was practiced in the Turkish Empire, and that there were harems, despotic rulers seemingly subject to no laws, and an exotic aura to things "Oriental"—whether in spices, bronze hanging lamps, exquisite rugs, belly dancers, bedizened camels, or the tales of Scheherazade—emphasized the differences between

Along the Gulf of Oman, one of the primary livelihoods is fishing. Dried fish and fishmeal are major exports of Oman. (Gurnee Dyer, recent)

East and West. All of this, added to the political rivalries, affected Western thought enormously and built a prejudice still rampant today.

Islam, the dominant faith of the modern Near East, is not simply a religion but a way of life. The Word of God, as conveyed to men by the prophet Muhammad and written down in the Holy Koran, is not altogether a doctrinal statement. It stipulates what the individual should be from birth to death, not in terms of an ideal only, but as a practical guide rooted in the experience of living in the Near East. Remarkable about the Koran is that its practice leads eventually to that ideal. For millions of people Islam is simple to follow, and the promise of salvation it extends to its followers goes far beyond the elaborations, rites, and promises of many other religions. But to Europeans the idea of the oneness of God, Islam's basic theme, subverts the Christian principle of the Trinity, for it denies the divinity of Christ although accepting the role of Jesus as a prophet. Furthermore, the Koran does not oppose polygamy. And it indicates that the Muslim, i.e., one who has submitted to God, has a duty to oppose the non-Muslim. Even prior to the Turks' dominance, the Arabs and their followers, who were converted from paganism to Islam, came into conflict with Christians doctrinally and eventually militarily, as the Crusades and the conquest of Spain demonstrate. To the West, the Koran was far from a holy book; it was a statement of paganism.

In these more enlightened times we know that atrocities, ruthlessness, sensuous rites, political aggrandizement, and all the other attributes assigned to the people of the Near East were qualities applied also to the West by Near Eastern inhabitants. Historically, then, these two great cultural traditions, both of which sprang from the same civilized root, have misunderstood and warred with one another. The conflict continues today on other matters and for other reasons. But it has a depth that goes far beyond physical conflict and misunderstanding of the other's way of life. In some ways it can be understood best as the age-old confrontation between Western reason and Eastern faith.

The evolution of Western conceptions of the cosmos and man's place in it has been one that has shifted man's position from being in the midst of a God-centered universe to one in which man conceives of God only as a philosophical possibility on the one side, and, on the other, of the universe as a material entity capable of being measured and subjected to universal laws of physical time and space. In this concept man is the product of biological evolution, a primate selected out by his capability to adapt to a physical and cultural environment. Through impersonal laws, economic-technological ideologies, egalitarianism imposed by authority, and a basic rootlessness, Western man increasingly regulates his society by technological values. Few Western representatives in the Near East profess Christianity, whether businessmen, the press, or Foreign Service agents. Their actions are generally related to economic and political affairs.

Western man has tended to view Near Eastern cultures as exotic, rooted in values opposed to or unheard of in the West and therefore to be enlightened by conversion or benign conquest, or as something to be studied academically as one would study disease or electricity, and then draw conclusions by so-called objective methods. Thus the human experience is completely left out, or, if retained, refers more to the sensational than to the ecology of daily and historical life.

But what is the true image of Near Eastern cultures? There are many. Perhaps the composite picture—the mosaic—is the medium for our understanding.

Initially, there is the geographical premise. The Near East is generally an arid region. Only 5 percent of the total region is cultivable, which means that permanent settlement is confined to strictly prescribed areas: to alluvial stretches of fertility, such as the valley of the Tigris-Euphrates, in rainless regions; or to the rainy coasts of the Levant and the

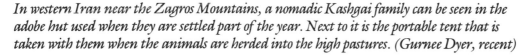

In western Iran near the Zagros Mountains, a nomadic Kashgai family can be seen in the adobe hut used when they are settled part of the year. Next to it is the portable tent that is taken with them when the animals are herded into the high pastures. (Gurnee Dyer, recent)

foothill countries of Mazanderan; or to simple oases or upland valley plots. Much of the cultivable land is irrigated land, and it is probably true that at least half of the agricultural production of the Near East is from irrigated soils. The produce is largely cereal grains, with fruit and vegetables for local consumption. Today, market crops such as sugar cane, tobacco, and cotton vie for and even appropriate lands that normally produce subsistence crops and they are making some Near Eastern countries more and more dependent on food imports.

Nearly 80 percent of Near Eastern people are involved in agriculture, so that populations concentrate heavily where agricultural activity results in large production. Cities such as Damascus, Medina, Baghdad, and Shiraz are not only famed centers of religion, learning, and commerce, but they are also viable centers in areas of agricultural production. Such cities attract the products of pastoralists and here the hair, hides, meat, and rugs of pastoral enterprise are exchanged for manufactured objects and agricultural goods; such exchanges also go on below the city level, in villages.

The characteristic city of the Near East is most likely one whose wealth derives from commerce. The Near East generally lacks natural resources, except for oil, a product that has only recently been exploited. Its position between inner Asia, Africa, and Europe has great advantages. The Near Eastern city traditionally has been the seat of a merchant class that deals in products indigenous to the Near East or from regions far beyond. The merchants are wealthy patrons of culture and they are sophisticated in extra-local affairs. The fate of ships and caravans being dependent on the skill of Arab crews and caravan leaders, the merchant is as much concerned with local support as with distant markets. Thus his sophistication goes far beyond a knowledge of world affairs.

Connected with commerce are the splendors of Near Eastern craftsmanship. Urban crafts are generally carried on by families through the generations. Characteristically, the shop is at the same time a retail outlet, a factory, and a place of residence. Frequently the crafts segregate along particular streets or areas; thus, streets of copper wares, rugs, basketwork, ceramics, jewelry, and cloth are an integral part of the Near Eastern city.

The Near Eastern city has certain features that show its role as a point in a commercial network and as a seat of the political control of princes or dynasties. The Islamic city usually centers on the mosque. Often there is a great central mosque and many smaller ones distributed throughout the city. Associated with the mosques are the religious schools. Near the great mosques are the central bazaars, or markets, which include storehouses and shops separated according to merchandise. Here, too, the merchant class has its large houses. The representatives of the Islamic religion usually live in this area as well. The favorite place of social interaction between merchants is the *hammam*, or bath, which is apparently modeled after those in the Classical world. Beyond the bazaar are the essentially residential quarters divided by ethnic or religious affinity—a quarter for Coptic Christians, Jews, Armenians, Assyrians, and so on. Many of these quarters are walled, and people have carried on the basic traditions of their own way of life within these confines. Jewish synagogues, Christian churches, and sects of Islam are all viable within

(text continued on page 97)

Coffee is the traditional drink of hospitality in the Bedouin world, where it is made
by the men; these gracefully spouted brass pots are from Saudi Arabia, Kuwait, and
Dubai. Height: (left) 14 inches; (center) 10 inches; (right) 12 inches

The Torah, or Pentateuch, the first five books of the Bible, is the oldest historical statement of a people whose origins are in the ancient Near East. The original Hebrew script has changed over the centuries but the substance and actual meaning have remained unaltered. The decorative crowns for the sacred scroll are meant to crown and adorn the sacred word of God. Height: (Torah) 37 inches; (crown) 16 inches

This carved stand is used for consulting and displaying the Koran, which is regarded by Muslims as the final and complete word of God, as revealed to the prophet Muhammad. Small, simple stands can be used privately in the home or enormous, elaborate ones can be seen as major equipment in the mosque. The nineteenth-century copper vessel is from Islamic India. Height: (stand) 28½ inches (vessel), 18 inches

Prayer rugs are woven in Iran and Turkey mostly by peasants and nomads. The design (visible in the top rug) often features in a geometric pattern the mihrab, *or mosque alcove set in the wall facing Mecca. The rug is placed on the floor facing the* gibla *(direction of Mecca) for praying toward the sacred city. The top rug is from a village near Konya in Turkey; the bottom one from the Taurus Mountains of Turkey. Dimensions: (top) 65 inches long, 45 inches wide; (bottom) 62 inches long, 38¹/₂ inches wide*

OPPOSITE:

Turkish boys, like boys everywhere, liked to emulate their fathers. This early nineteenth-century military costume was worn by a little boy whose father wore a similar outfit imported from outside Turkey. Collected by the author in Istanbul, the uniform has bullet pouches with ten false wooden bullets capped with silver; the hat is curly sheepskin lined with blue silk; the coat is wool and the vest is blue silk. The uniform is trimmed with silver tinsel ribbon. Length: (coat) 31¹/₂ inches; (hat) 6 inches

Amulets and charms are a common type of Turkish jewelry; this silver necklace,
with a 4½-inch amulet case, was worn by a woman in Geyre, Turkey.

OPPOSITE:

The rich mines of Armenia supplied gold, silver, and copper to western Asia for
thousands of years, and Armenian craftsmen achieved a high level of metalworking
skills. The silver belt came from Van, and the filigree tray, cups, and plates date from
nineteenth-century Aleppo. Length: (belt) 30¼ inches; (tray) 19½ inches

OPPOSITE:

Both men and women in Afghanistan wear elaborate jewelry of gold, silver, and brass set with lapis lazuli and other semiprecious stones. This Pushtun neck crescent of openwork silver was purchased in a Kabul bazaar. Width: 9 inches

These two women's anklets from Nezwah, North Oman, are hinged with a clasp and closed with a pin. Both are about five inches in diameter of hollow silver with geometric relief patterns.

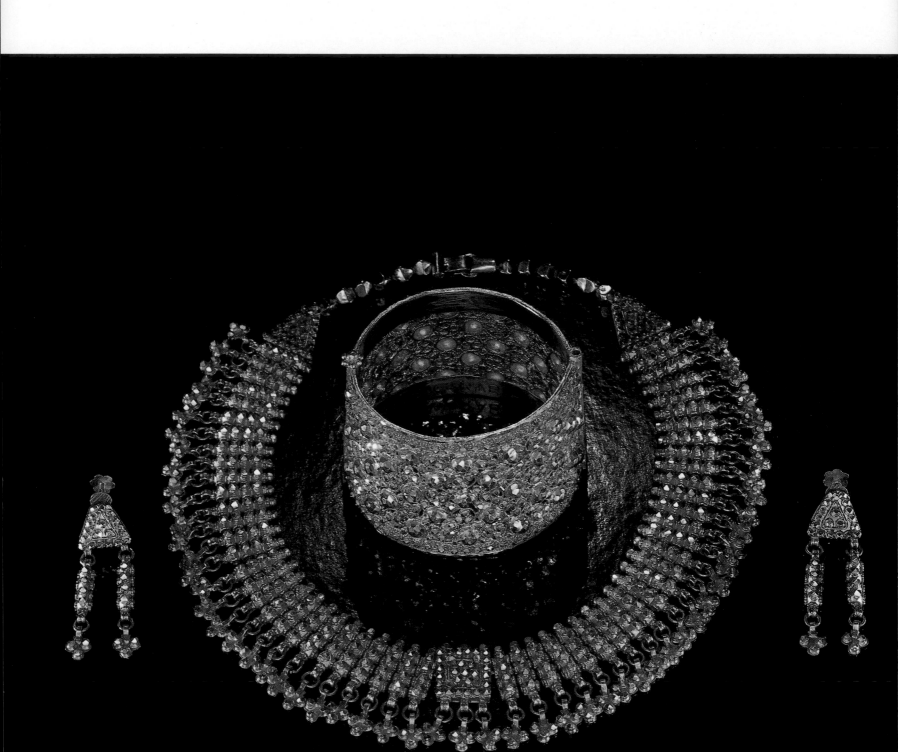

Omani women wear silver hair cones tied to the ends of their braids; each cone is filled with wool dipped in perfume. This piece, like most jewelry worn in Oman, was created by a Yemeni silversmith. Length: 4 inches

OPPOSITE:

A Jewish goldsmith in Aden, South Yemen, created this very fine twentieth-century necklace, bracelet, and earrings from cast and faceted gold. The design is said to be similar to jewelry made in ancient Israel. Length: (necklace) 15½ inches; (earrings) 2 inches. Width: (bracelet) 1½ inches

(text continued from page 84)

the segregated areas of the city. Indeed, traditionally each quarter is responsible for policing itself and maintaining its own law and order. Frequently there are food bazaars within a quarter. The quarter's debt to the larger city is mostly in terms of taxes collected locally by the heads of the quarter. In times when the collective city has needs, consultation with the quarter leaders may occur and joint action is the rule.

Outside the residential zone are the areas where temporary visitors might come to stay in caravanserais or where the outside bazaars are located. In these outside bazaars pastoral nomads might sell their animals or animal products. Caravans are made up or disbanded here. Characteristic also of these "suburbs" are the vast cemeteries, many of which are centered around the tombs of saints or holy men. Although these cemeteries are generally outside the city walls, this is not always so, and much difficulty has occurred historically as people have expanded into these cities of the dead.

In the past, government has depended to some extent on the power of individuals or royal houses to impose their will on the countryside. It is not surprising, therefore, that the citadel, a fortification on a natural elevation, was often the symbol of government. Near the citadel, even perhaps surrounding it, was the royal city, which included the monarch's palace, the residences of the court, and the barracks for the military bodyguard. Gardens surrounding the royal residence, often separating the complex from the functional buildings of government, were also part of the royal city.

Rulership in the Near East has been closely affiliated with religion. This was no less true in King David's day in ancient Israel than later in the traditional Islamic countries. At the heart of government is the *ulama*, a council of wise men representing various backgrounds, all of whom are trained in religion and can give advice on government to the ruler. In some sense, the *ulama* represents a link between the people and the leaders. An important figure is the *qadi*, or judge, who might be appointed by the ruler but who acts according to the interpretation of the Koranic law made by the local *ulama*. In terms of the physical city, mosque-palace-military (the last marked the ruler's capability of enforcing his rule) form one structure. However, the merchants usually have spokesmen, or representatives, on the *ulama*, and a local *ulama* representing them may also have its influence.

Important is that the Koran places great emphasis on the behavior of the individual. Everyone is equal before Allah, whatever his secular status. Thus the judgment of the *ulama* is as much a comment on the individual as it is an interpretation of the Koran. Not society is responsible for the individual's actions, as some modern people would argue, but the individual himself. Accordingly, self-will, freedom of choice, and personal responsibility are as much a part of the Muslim's world view as they are for Christians or Jews. This individualism has a significant influence on the character of the Muslim house. In the traditional urban quarter one wanders down streets with houses on both sides; they have no windows on the first story and screened balconies on the second. Access to

This silver dress ornament decorated with blue beads and turquoise is from the Pushtun tribe, and was made in Gardez, Afghanistan. Width: 5 inches

the house is through a door that opens on a vestibule and then to a winding passage leading into a courtyard beyond which may be a reception area for the visitor. The men's quarters, kitchen, and often service areas are nearby, the women's quarters more remote. Whether wealthy or not, a sharp division is made between what is social, i.e., necessary, in the normal nonbusiness intercourse of the individual's life, and what is familial, i.e., directly related to the life of the individual as a member of a biologically related unit. The house is basically familial in nature—an extension of the individual and therefore private. In consequence, clear-cut physical divisions separate the social and the familial.

Most people in the Near East live in villages. Basically, the villager is a peasant; that is, most village land is not owned by the villager but by the government or landlords. High rentals, taxes, and the vagaries of the seasons, which traditional technology could not deal with, have made village farming difficult. The villager is rooted to the land, and movement away from difficulties, as is possible for the nomad, is almost impossible for him. In consequence, villagers are exploitable and, more than any other group, have been the most poorly off. For this reason land reform has been one of the major developments of the revolutionary governments that have emerged since World War II.

The typical village consists of a group of mud-walled, flat-roofed houses, irregularly placed about one another, some of two stories. The houses, set in the midst of a walled compound into which animals can be driven in the evening, usually have a kitchen room, two sleeping rooms (or a divided sleeping room), a central social or reception room, storage rooms, ovens, mangers, perhaps a tower for pigeons, and sometimes a well in the courtyard. Groves of trees—date palms in the south, almond, walnut, pistachio, and poplar in the north—are part of the village landscape, providing both shade and fruit. The village is set in the midst of fields. When a man bequeaths some share of land to all his sons, the land becomes fractionalized because of inheritance practices. Often a peasant may work one large field near the house and three or more much smaller ones scattered over the village holdings. A village mosque and perhaps a small schoolroom are the public buildings. The village well provides both water and a place for exchanging gossip. In general, the village is self-sufficient, perhaps more so in the past when village potters, weavers, and smiths provided the necessities. Today, of course, manufactured goods produced by national industries, the emphasis on money as the medium of exchange, and the pressure to grow market crops have reduced village self-sufficiency enormously.

Whereas the city-village settlement pattern is based upon a small fraction of the total Near Eastern land, pastoral nomads are widely found. They fall into two broad economic groups: desert Arabs, who move seasonally across wide stretches of the Syro-Arabian desert; and mountain pastoralists, who seasonally ascend and descend the mountain slopes transhumantly, particularly those of the Zagros Mountains. The desert group emphasizes camels and some horses, and the mountain group sheep, goats, and cattle. But there are variations all through these regions. Both groups place great importance on the abilities of the individual, and individual prowess is a matter of high prestige. Chiefs and sheikhs retain authority when they are successful as arbitrators, warriors, and possessors of economic wealth. Egalitarianism is particularly important, for the emphasis on the individual calls for a role for those deserving a say in affairs. Chiefs, therefore, spend a considerable

In tribal country in western Iran, a Kashgai drives a sledge over grain on a threshing platform. Threshing goes on day and night, with the people working in shifts. After the husks are separated from the grain, the grain is winnowed. (Jean and Franc Shor, recent)

The Kerbela Mosque is a splendid example of Islamic architecture and is a major Shiite Muslim shrine. The Shiites constitute a branch of Islam that believes that the leadership of the Muslim community rightfully belongs to an Imam descended from Muhammad through his daughter Fatima and son-in-law Ali. Half of Iraq and most of Iran is Shiite. (c. 1900)

period of time in consultation with the representatives of the men of the group. In social organization, the characteristic family is dominated by the oldest male, and through his line the inheritance passes. The family is exogamous. Among the Arabs, ideally all married sons live near the father, and through time a lineage develops relating each generation to a founding ancestor. These ancestral relationships also relate lineage to lineage, resulting in a collection of generationally, or historically, related people who speak the same language, acknowledge the same ancestors, and seasonally follow the same pastoral routes. This large grouping acknowledges a dominant lineage, that of the tribal chief. The residential units are the camps in which the famous black tents are found. These are made of goat and camel hair and are divided into two parts—women on the left, men on the right. Although women do the cooking, the men take pride in preparing coffee for which they have a special brazier and traditional implements. Sharing coffee is a mark of hospitality.

The sexual division of labor is quite clear. Women do the domestic tasks; men take care of the herds. Raiding for camels and horses was standard practice among the bedouin of Arabia as a means of regulating herd size and giving an opportunity for increas-

Family ties are of great importance in Iran, especially among nomads and the urban upper class. Extended families are common, and endogamous marriage is the preferred arrangement. This photograph is probably of an upper-class urban family in the courtyard of its house. (late 19th century)

Bread is being sold by weight at this Persian bakery. (late 19th century)

ing wealth, which the normal growth of the herds did not permit. Seasonal movement is fairly strictly prescribed by adherence to traditional routes and pastures in both mountain and desert pastoralism.

Some seasonal agriculture is practiced by some of the mountain groups, but in general farming is looked down upon. The Iranian government has practiced antinomadic policies in an effort to convert the nomads to permanent village farming and as a means of enforcing authority. It has been only partially successful in doing so, in part because of a basic contempt for the kind of settled existence that is opposite to the nomadic world view, and in part because of the fear of government control.

Apart from the pastoral nomadic regions and the agricultural areas, certain places such as the highlands of Armenia, the Ionian coasts of Anatolia, the swamps of Basra, the blind delta of Seistan, and the hill fastnesses of northern Syria, Anatolia, and Iran are primarily areas of isolation; or, as in the case of Ionia and Armenia, they are important marginal regions serving as links to non-Near Eastern cultures. The isolated areas are frequently refugee sanctuaries; historically, other ways of life, languages, and people, as well as sects of various religions such as the Druses, Yezidis, and certain Christian groups, have survived there, having disappeared elsewhere.

The second premise beside the physical and cultural geography is the historical. History confirms what geography has outlined. Almost as far back as we have records there have been village farmers, pastoral nomads, isolated and marginal cultures, and urban merchants. Commerce and dynastic rule have acted as cohesive forces between these disparities, as has religion. Religion in the Near East is, of course, strikingly different from that in any other area of Asia, for its emphasis upon individual presentation before deity is not only related to personal belief but to the ethics of daily life.

A group of Circassian women pose languidly in this studio photograph. Many Circassians, a people of the Caucasus, settled in Turkish territory during Ottoman rule or were brought in as slaves. They are now mostly acculturated. Circassian women were thought to be very beautiful and were sought after by wealthy Muslims for their harems. (late 19th century)

There have been many books written about the origins of the Near Eastern ethical faiths: Judaism, Zoroastrianism, Christianity, and Islam. One thing is clear—no one way of life was the genesis of these religions. Quite the contrary, it was the varied ethnographic mixtures that provided the setting for the birth of the ideas leading to monotheism and the relationship of man to a single God. As outlined previously, the rise of the early Near Eastern civilizations was possible primarily because of the success of intensive agricultural practice in the Fertile Crescent areas. These civilizations were marked ideologically by a pantheon of deities, all of whom in one way or another shared the powers of nature. They created the world and all that is in it. Then man himself was created to work for the gods who disdained the mundane daily activities of subsistence seeking, which they paradoxically needed as much as man. The concept of "I," that is, the vitalism of things that gave them their special character, revealed a powerful animism underlying their world view. This is still found today among peoples of the Near East. The world of the Near Eastern cultivator and the pastoral nomad is one which, though giving due allegiance to Islam, still conceives of spirits, ghosts, demons, and the efficacy of amulets. The reader of *The Arabian Nights*—stories derived mostly from pre-Islamic tales—comes into contact with genii, magicians, sorcerers, and other supernatural powers. In one village I was shown a newborn baby; later I was warned that should the baby die during the night, it would be because I had put the evil eye on it! Such stories can be repeated throughout the Near East.

These animistic accounts signify that Near Eastern people conceive of a world that has both natural and supernatural parts to it. Knowing this, everything can be classified as belonging to one or another part. Furthermore, the events of the day or year can be placed in a timeless frame of cause and effect: the evil eye exists; the stranger sees the newborn baby; the baby dies; the stranger must have the evil eye; do not show a newborn baby to strangers. Or, demons walk straight lines; walk down crooked streets and demons cannot follow. Or, the Koran is the Word of God; therefore a page from the Koran pasted over a wound brings the Word in contact with the wound; a cure will occur; if not, the victim has not been worthy of God!

The Bible is filled with stories in which the supernatural plays a role at critical times: Saul visits the Witch of Endor; Aaron's staff turns into a serpent; the blood of the lamb painted on certain doors causes the Angel of Death to pass over; the Hebrews dance around the calf of gold as soon as Moses leaves them. Trance, dancing rites, self-flagellation, and prayer repetition are practiced by dervishes, Iranian students, Christian devotees, and Jewish sects according to their individual group practice. Pilgrimages to holy places, made sacred by events between deity and man, are timeless in the Near East. The Sumerians went to the sacred grove at Nippur; the Jews repeat rites at the Wailing Wall; Muslims make pilgrimages to Mecca. In all these things, benefits for the believer are obtained and means of functioning now and in future insured.

Gypsies have lived in Persia since the sixth century, and number in the thousands. Gypsy men were often skillful blacksmiths, while the women sometimes earned money fortune-telling or belly dancing, roles that proper Muslim women could not fulfill. (late 19th century)

This old tourist album photograph is described as "where the Jordan meets the Dead Sea."
The salt content of the Dead Sea is about 24 percent, or seven times that of the ocean;
consequently, swimmers and boats float like corks. (negative signed by Langaki, probably 1870s)

Between the need to classify the world according to form and genesis, and to relate the events of daily life to simple understandable cause and effect relationships, the rise of Near Eastern religions has a basis in the known world. They were not the product of an outside philosophy or cosmology, but something shared since prehistoric times. Today, Western materialism, whether in terms of capitalism or Marxism, confronts only the surface aspects of Near Eastern faith, and Westerners tend to see only what is obvious.

In this context, ancient Near Eastern paganism, with its pantheism arising out of an animistic foundation, can be considered to be a means of classifying the powers of the world, a means of explanation as valid for the time and place as seem to be the scientific explanations today. In the ancient agricultural communities, pantheism as expressed in temples and by priests, monthly rites, sacrifices, processions, idols and icons, and repetitive doctrine was the nucleus of the state. By the time of the Assyrians and Chaldeans (1000–550 B.C.), the weight of ritual and ceremonial elaboration had become so great that it lost its meaning; and ritual was complex, costly, and empty.

Judaism was originally the product of pastoral-nomadic ideology, according to historians of theology. The patriarchal cycles of Abraham, Isaac, and Jacob, with their stories of herding, of seeking pasture, of camp, and of the simplicity of a life where wealth was counted by number of animals and number of sons, are familiar to the student of Near Eastern pastoralism. It should be noted that pastoralists classify their world more in terms of animistic vitalism than of pantheism. Quite simply, there is good luck and bad luck, much and little, hot and cold, water and no water, far and near, friend and enemy, old and young, courage and cowardice, advantage and disadvantage. These are qualities in everyday life, made perfectly understandable by that life. Some scholars, as well as political officers, have called the Arab bedouin childlike because of this polarity of world view:

They were incorrigibly children of the idea, feckless and colour-blind, to whom body and spirit were for ever and inevitably opposed. Their mind was strange and dark, full of depressions and exaltations, lacking in rule, but with more of ardour and more fertile in belief than any other in the world.

(T. E. Lawrence, Revolt in the Desert.)

In this context, the explanation not only for the existence of things but why they function as they do is given quite readily: courage is acknowledged because it is the opposite of cowardice; a time of plenty occurs because it is in contrast to a time of nonplenty; the childless man has no way of preserving his name, "he is as nothing"; but children give his name a kind of immortality, "he is a man among men."

The prophet Zoroaster, who lived around 600 B.C., saw the world as a battleground between the forces of goodness and light led by Ahura-Mazda, and those of evil and darkness led by Ahriman. Zoroaster was apparently a pastoralist, who in his world view acknowledged the essential polarity of his culture's ideology. It is no coincidence that in Zoroastrianism ritual fire is the principal element, for it is a symbol of man's desire to fight on the side of purity and goodness for the salvation of the world. Once the principal religion of Iran, it now has very few adherents—a minority in Iran in Yazd and Kerman, and the Parsis of India. In part, this is because the Muslims who conquered Iran could never reconcile Zoroastrian emphasis on fire as a ritual element while doctrinally admitting the struggle against Satan's wiles.

Judaism admits the polarity of good and evil as demonstrated in the Book of Job. But Judaism is not a faith of polarities unless men and God can be taken as such. Ultimately any creation myth has to come to grips with ultimate cause, or, in effect, the existence of something before polarity. To the herder, there seems to be an active male principle and a more passive female principle. Male and female are necessary for life, but it is the male who seeks the female and not the reverse. It is no coincidence that there is a maleness to the God of Abraham, of Jesus, and of Muhammad. God is taken as an active principle, so powerful, so universal that he is beyond polarity and yet at the same time is responsible for that polarity. God in this conception is both supernatural, that is, beyond secular comprehension yet manifest in all existence, and natural in that the material or comprehended world is proof of the existence of God.

In the Torah, we see this sense of God's ultimate being. He is the creator of all, as in the first chapter of Genesis: he punishes (Sodom and Gomorrah), saves (Noah), directs (Abraham), warns (Moses), and gives means by which man can act on earth (the Mosaic Law). In the stories of the wanderings in Sinai, and the period of Judges and Kings, we are made aware of the power of paganism, as again and again the Hebrew leaders warn the populace of the terms of the Covenant. King Solomon builds a vast temple to house the Ark of the Covenant, and its ritual nature comes very close to the pagan rites common throughout the sedentary Near East, so much so that the burning of the Temple by the Babylonians is regarded as the final disaster by the captive Hebrews. It takes Jeremiah and Isaiah to reinforce the ancient belief that God is wherever the individual believer is and that temples literally are not worthy of God.

The Achaemenid Persians, who were the Indo-European-speaking conquerors of the old Semitic states of the Near East, ruled from northern India to Egypt and the Aegean Sea. The most powerful of the ancient empires, it consolidated much of the learning of the ancient civilizations and internationalized its realm by permitting local beliefs and institutions to continue under the state cult which proclaimed the essential divinity of the reigning emperor. The Hebrews, for example, were allowed to return to Jerusalem. It is in this period that some of the finest Hebrew writing may have occurred, including the composition of some of the Psalms. Essentially this represents the final amalgam of a basically pastoral nomadic world view with that of the sedentary world without reversion to paganism.

After the conquests of the Persians by Alexander of Macedon (357–323 B.C.), the Hellenistic monarchy of the Seleucids and the smaller kingdoms, like those of the Attalids

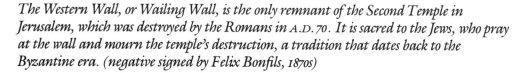

The Western Wall, or Wailing Wall, is the only remnant of the Second Temple in Jerusalem, which was destroyed by the Romans in A.D. 70. It is sacred to the Jews, who pray at the wall and mourn the temple's destruction, a tradition that dates back to the Byzantine era. (negative signed by Felix Bonfils, 1870s)

The Jaffa Gate of Jerusalem, one of the most famous of its gates, is shown in this early photograph taken by the Near Eastern photographer Felix Bonfils, who operated a studio in Beirut during the 1870s. (Although Bonfils signed all the negatives produced in his studio, as he did this one, some of the photographs were taken by his assistants.)

of Pergamum, maintained paganism; both state cults and a multiplicity of animistic faiths, numbered only by the number of different cultures, marked the landscape. Judaism had its sectarian divisions, as the Dead Sea scrolls attest rather dramatically.

With Rome's conquest of the Levant, Egypt, Anatolia, and Armenia, the Hellenistic pagan cults continued to flourish, but the Messianic sects of Judaism became dominated by one whom the Muslims later recognized as the eleventh prophet from the time of Abraham, Jesus of Nazareth. In Jesus, we can again recognize the effort to escape paganism by preaching the one God of ancient Israel. The faith of Jesus is clearly a revolt against the religious paraphernalia created by sedentary life and the hybridization natural to a Palestine that stands geographically on the high road north and south, east and west. There is a strong suggestion that the young man raised in a sedentary world of villages returned to the desert for a time. Little is known of Jesus' middle years, but his actions in the last two seem more related to the polarities of pastoralism than to the taxonomies of sedentary farming. This can be partially explained by his probable access to Messianic teachings, like those symbolized by John the Baptist. However much rooted in Judaism, the world view that includes the Gentiles and emphasizes the individuality of man in his relationship to deity is, as in bedouin life, pan-tribal.

When Christianity became the state religion of Rome, it developed a sectarianism in a number of centers, ending with the schisms that plague its unity into modern day. There was the development of the Greek Orthodox Church in Byzantium (Constantinople), seat of the Eastern Roman Empire. There were amalgams with Christianity and influences from older pagan beliefs in Alexandria (the Coptic Church) and Antioch (seat of Syrian Christianity). By the fourth century, the Nestorian Christians were finding sanctuary in Iran and centuries later came to China. At the same time Armenian Christianity, which is one of the oldest Christian sects to survive, came into being.

The Jews had been dispersed when Jerusalem was looted after a revolt against Rome in A.D. 71 and shortly after the successful conclusion of the siege of Masada by the Romans. Most Jews were established in Europe, particularly in Spain (Sephardim) and in Eastern Europe (Ashkenazim). However, Jews stayed in Asia in Yemen, Iran, India, and Georgia. Some returned to Palestine in Ottoman times. Now, of course, the modern state of Israel is a response to the Psalm, "Can I forget thee, Oh Jerusalem."

The most important development in the Near East after the division of the Roman Empire and its gradual demise was the appearance of Islam. Muhammad (c. A.D. 570–632) lost his mother at the age of six and lived apparently as a shepherd close to his birthplace Mecca in western Arabia; later in his youth, he worked on caravans traveling south to Yemen or north to Syria. He married the widow Khadija, who was fifteen years his senior and active in the trade of which he became a part. Apparently even as a boy Muhammad had dreams of events difficult to interpret. He seems to have been a thoughtful, rather introspective, person given to quiet contemplation of his world. It was a quarrelsome, warlike world, basically pagan and caught in the failings of the worn-out empires of Sassanian Persia and Byzantine Rome. Clearly in any search for meaning to life, to human action, to self-identity, the experiences vividly portrayed all about him, both in Mecca and in his journeys, raised more questions than answers.

It is certain that Muhammad found in the mountains surrounding Mecca the solitude necessary to give his thoughts focus. As Zoroaster perceived his vision of man and God in the solitude of the desert, as Moses talked with God on Mount Sinai, and as Jesus saw the whole earth from the mountaintop in the wilderness, so Muhammad on Mount Hira had a vision of the Archangel Gabriel and heard the Word of God:

> *Recite in the name of thy God who*
> *   created man from coagulated blood*
> *Recite! Thy Lord is merciful*
> *Who by the pen has taught mankind*
> *The things they did not know!*

At first filled with self-doubt and fearful of dreams of self-deceit, Muhammad remained silent while he wrestled with his convictions. At last he realized the reality of what had happened to him and began to preach of the oneness of God, of his universality:

God is the light of heaven and earth. His light may be compared to a niche which contains a lamp, the lamp within glass, and the glass like a star of pearl. It is lit from the oil of an olive tree of neither east nor west but is blessed. Its oil is so lucid that it might shine even without the touch of fire. Light upon light, God's light guides those who believe in him.

Muhammad preached of a final day of judgment; of man's individual responsibility for his own conduct under God; of the prophets Abraham, Moses, and Jesus, who had already spoken the Word of God. He spoke of God's love and repeated the formula known to all Muslims:

> *Praise be to Allah, the Lord of Mankind,*
> *The Merciful, the Compassionate,*
> *Master of the Day of Judgment.*
> *We worship Thee and ask for thy Guidance*
> *Guide us to do what is right*
> *To follow the path of those Thou hast favored,*
> *Not to follow the path of those*
> *   who anger Thee or have gone astray.*

Muhammad required of all those who submitted to God (Islam: submission to God; Muslim: one who has submitted to God) that they follow the teaching of the Koran by professing the faith—God's revelations that Muhammad uttered as God's prophet. Fundamental to this teaching were five moral and ritual duties: to observe the faith; to pray

Three Persian women on the deck of a ship wear the chador, *or traditional robe of Muslim women that covers the body from head to toe. In the past, veiled women mostly came from the urban upper classes of Persia (Iran). Today a reversal is taking place; the westernized city-dwellers are abandoning the* chador *while the lower classes, and to a lesser extent rural classes, are taking up the practice. In Iran before the revolution, it was not uncommon to see a sophisticated city woman wearing a* chador *over a miniskirt. (late 19th century)*

109

Chiefs of the Kashgai tribe in Iran begin a feast of rice, game, lamb, and other Persian dishes. Note the combination of western and traditional Iranian dress, a common sight in twentieth-century Iran. (J.B. Thorpe, mid 20th century)

A young shopkeeper in Damascus rests in the shade. One of the oldest continuously inhabited cities in the world, Damascus lies on an ancient caravan route and is a market point for the Bedouins of the Syrian desert. It is a city filled with fine old Arab houses, fountains, and souqs (bazaars) famous for their brassware, silk, and fragrant carved wood.

daily (there are five traditional times, at dawn, noon, afternoon, sunset, night); to give alms out of mercy and charity; to fast during the daytime of the month of Ramadan, the month when the Koran was revealed; and to make a pilgrimage to Mecca (*hajj*) once in one's lifetime, if possible.

Mecca was a center of paganism in those days; even the Kaaba, later the Muslim holy of holies, was a pagan shrine. So many pilgrims came to this pagan center that it was very profitable for the merchants there. Muhammad's antipagan preaching enraged the commercial rulers of the city, and they made every effort to stop Muhammad and his increasing number of followers. At last, in the year 622, Muhammad and his followers fled to the city of Medina, a handsome place set in the midst of a date-palm oasis. Muslims count their era from this hegira, or migration, from Mecca.

Years of further preaching followed and of military campaigns that culminated in a return to Mecca in 630, which then, as the place where the Word of God was heard, became a holy city. The band of converts enlarged more and more and became a brotherhood to whom Muhammad preached the laws governing the relationships among men and women under God. At his death in A.D. 632, much of the Arabian peninsula was converted to Islam. The government of the people of the state was no longer secular but Islamic, and political leaders had to submit to the authority of religious law. In fact, the head of the Islamic state was known as the caliph or successor (to Muhammad). To this day, via the *ulama* institution, Koranic law influences secular governments among Muslim nations of the Near East.

After Muhammad's death a division occurred in the leadership between those who thought that caliphate succession should be elective and not hereditary, the Sunni, and those who felt that it should be hereditary. The latter picked Muhammad's nephew and son-in-law Ali, and took the name of Shia, or partisans of Ali. Ali was murdered by the Sunni, and his sons, Hasan and Husain, were later killed. Ali has a tomb at Najaf and Husain at Karbala, both in Iraq, and these are among the holiest shrines of Islam for the Shiites. Shiism took hold in Iraq and most notably in Iran. The concept of the imam, in effect a descendant of the line of Ali, has various forms in Shiism, but there are deviations, some believing that the imam is divinely appointed and has succeeded in every way Muhammad himself. There is a messianic quality about Shia for some accept a second coming of a Mahdi (guided one). In fact, several candidates have appeared historically, such as the Mahdi of the Sudan.

The Sunni are regarded as more orthodox and are firm followers of the Sharia or Koranic law. There is a secularity about some of their interpretations of the Koran that contrasts with the Shia doctrine. However, Sufism, the mysticism of Islam, is rooted in Sunni. Sufism emphasizes that oneness with God is not simply an act of faith but an immersion in God's tangible love. The literature of the Sufis is among the richest contributions of Islam to the world. No one reading the writings of the martyr al-Hallaj, the autobiography of al-Ghazali, or the poems of Hafiz or Sadi can be unmoved.

Arab unity gave the Muslims a military capability which, coupled with an augmenting group of converts of other regions, made possible the rapid conquest of kingdoms to the east and west. The Battle of Tours in France, in 732, one hundred years after Muhammad's death, brought their western expansion to an end; to the east, after conquering Sind and the southern Punjab in India, they seemed to have run out of steam, much like Alexander. All of the Near East but western Anatolia and Armenia was under Muslim rule.

What followed was the usual split-up as sectarianism and local separatist movements grew in momentum. The control of the caliphate by the Abbasids centered in Baghdad, marked by the rule of the famous Harun al-Rashid, was a highwater mark since Baghdad was an international center and seat of Arab learning; but unity soon collapsed. The story of the various countries of the Near East is one of invasion, particularly by the Turks and Mongols, of efforts to throw off the rule of the various dynasties, of periods of great cultural flowering like that of the Safavids of Iran, but never of a unity as in the early years following the Prophet's death.

In our own time, the exponents of Western thought are no longer the missionaries but the scientists, engineers, and agnostic, if not atheistic, politicians. It is beyond the scope of this book to explain this history of intellectual thought in the West. Christianity, hopelessly crucified on its sectarian cross, and Judaism, just now recovering from the Holocaust and striving to keep its small state safe, are no longer viable competitors to Islam; only Western material positivism is. The outcries from exponents of the Islamic tradition in today's world are symptoms of an inner struggle in the Near East.

Historically, there seems to have been always an interplay between the pastoral nomadic discovery of self-identity and the sedentary farmers' need to integrate the old with the new. Whereas the farmer may respond by multiplying the complexity of his world view, the pastoralist seems determined on simplifying it. The fact that bedouin Arabs now use Islam to account for bad or good luck and all the other things over which they have no control demonstrates an adaptability far beyond that of the sophisticated young men of Beirut, Riyadh, or Damascus, who grasp eagerly at Western ways.

Hunters watch on the banks of the Jordan. The Jordan is almost impossible to navigate because of rapids, sandbars, and cascades. In places it meanders between two points more than three times longer than airline distance. (negative signed by Felix Bonfils, probably 1870s)

THE
DHARMA OF
INDIA

FOR THE WEST, THE STORY of the Indo-Pakistan subcontinent is dominated by the history of Englishmen living there over a span of more than three hundred years. The modern states of India, Pakistan, and Sri Lanka are justifiably proud of their own independence, both politically and culturally, but for the Westerner it is Great Britain and her institutions that dominate and provide a temporal bridge to an understanding of those states. For all three countries arose out of the colonial experience which saw Englishmen come as traders and stay as rulers. English is a lingua franca in south Asia, and there are over eight hundred words of Indian origin in use in the English language. This is symptomatic of the fact that the European experience there was by no means one-sided. As English invention and organization brought to an end the feudal, ancient character of life in the subcontinent, so Indian philosophy, crafts, and the opportunity of new horizons for Europeans changed the Western world view.

E. M. Forster's novel *A Passage to India*, which depicts the injustices foisted upon an Indian civil servant by Englishmen, has to be balanced with John Masters's experiences as an officer of a Gurkha regiment where mutual respect was the basis of substantive human relations. Rudyard Kipling's Gunga Din, the loyal water carrier in the wars of the northwest frontier, contrasts with the massacre at Amritsar when General Dyer ordered his men to fire on an Indian crowd. For every wrong, injustice, or hurt suffered on one side there was a right, an act of justice, kindness, or mercy on the other in equal proportion. No one can deny the injustice of colonialism and the natural right of a people to self-

Fatehpur Sikri near Agra, India, was abandoned in 1585, probably because of a poor water supply. It is a magnificent city of red sandstone buildings with an elaborate mosque and the famed Buland Darwaza—a gateway described as one of the noblest in the world. (B. M. De Cou, 1924)

determination, but the currents of history flowed from Europe to the East, and there was an inevitability about the search for markets and raw resources brought on by the Industrial Revolution. While Gandhi was a child of India, his voice was never stilled by the imperial achievement. What is remarkable about the British experience with India is that as the British gained respect for the Indian cultural heritage, so India gained respect for itself. What had once been divided and helpless now became unified.

It was the Indian past that awed European scholars as they gradually realized the immensity of the Indian heritage, a heritage that was largely unknown in eighteenth-century Europe. One must remember that Classical learning, with all its remarkable diversity and profundity, was nonetheless rooted in the cultures of ancient Greece and Rome, as well as in the Bible. This learning was the foundation of Western thought and paradoxically, for all its perspective, it was confining in its European ethnocentrism. Nevertheless, there were accounts in Herodotus and in the story of Alexander's eastern conquests as recounted by Arrian, Quintus Curtius Rufus, Diodoros, Justin, and Plutarch which described such facts as that the Indians had castes, held priests in high status, used elephants in battle, respected wise men, and had many cities often ruled by valiant kings. Such accounts could hardly do justice to the actuality but yet they had their value for they incorporated India to some extent in the Classical world for which Europeans had such respect.

There was another India, however, that had a particular place in the thoughts of Europeans from the time of Queen Elizabeth I and perhaps before. It was Hindustan... the Indies, a place of rich spices, carved treasures in jade, exotic wood, and ivory; ruby-bedecked maharajas, strutting peacocks, fierce tigers, multiheaded gods, fakirs on beds of nails, magicians whose boy assistants climbed on sky-suspended ropes and disappeared; a place of strange, often terrible, customs such as suttee (widow burning), child marriage, and thuggee (murder by thugs). Above all, there was the sense that the wise men of Hindustan must have cosmic knowledge far beyond the capacity of the West to understand. Of course some substantive reality about most of these visions of India exists, but the West for centuries failed and still fails, for the most part, to conceive of India as a civilization and not some cabinet of curiosities. Jules Verne in his *Around the World in Eighty Days* had his hero rescue the Indian princess from the funeral pyre. Katherine Mayo in *Mother India*, which was a bestseller in the 1920s, described the horrors of midwifery and the subjugation of Hindu women, and titillated the sadists in the West to purchase many editions. Lowell Thomas, as have other journalists, described the erotic scenes sculptured on the walls of the Black Pagoda of Konarak. And today, American policy labels India among the "developing" countries while Americans tourists, lamenting the hungry on the streets of Calcutta, see nothing of the verdant fields of the Punjab or Assam.

As with so much of Asia, India is that great paradox of contrasts between a reality conjured out of dream and a dream motivated by reality. In effect, even the simplest farmer amid the fields of the Deccan has a strong sense of past, present, and future, and of his place in the spatial manifestations of time. By now there have been hundreds of studies of the so-called Indian mind, revealing that Indians as a whole have a compelling sense of place in a larger structure, whether it be village, nation, or universe. The energizing aspect of this structural awareness is bound up in a word—dharma. Essentially, dharma refers to doing what has to be done in one's life, not simply as a drudgery or a labor of love but as something necessary and right. This was a major factor in Gandhi's Satyagraha, or peaceful resistance, which was critical in ending British rule in India. Gandhi considered violence as not only demeaning in the context of India, since it endangered the order of life, but un-Indian because it forced Indians to be what they were

This Muslim dancer (note the crescent and star in her hair) is probably also a prostitute. Dancers of different status entertained all levels of Indian society. In Indian dance, every gesture of the hands and fingers (the hastas and mudras respectively) has a specific meaning. With them, a dancer can actually tell a story or "recite" poetry. (A.S. Vernay, 1920s)

The Ganges River is especially sacred to the Hindus. Bathing and worshiping on its banks are considered incumbent upon the devout. On the Benares waterfront there are ascetics who stand all day with face and hands lifted toward the sun, or who lie prostrate or kneel before the river. The faithful wish to die in Benares, to be cremated on the banks of the river, and to have their ashes scattered across the waters. (above: B.M. De Cou, 1924; below: 1917)

not intended to be—a violent people who by physical power won their way. Such victories only led to more violence. Gandhi was much concerned about the relationship between morality and truth, and concluded that they were one and the same. If one acts morally, that is with the sense of dharma, one's actions are truthful and enduring. Because it was right that India should be free, the actions of Indians should be in keeping with that right. What is morally obvious does not need bloodshed to make it so, in fact, it would only obscure the truth of India's natural right to be free. A free India was envisioned as made up of many parts, a building constructed of all kinds of materials, each having an important place, the whole bound together by ahimsa or universal love. One can never imagine the Mahatma's agony when, in 1947, the British left India at last, and Muslims and Hindus slaughtered one another in one of the worst bloodbaths in history.

It is no coincidence that India has produced some of the greatest exponents of peace and understanding in the world: the Sakyamuni Buddha; Mahavira, founder of Jainism; the Emperor Asoka of the Mauryan dynasty, who officially abjured war; countless Hindus, Buddhists, Jains, and ultimately Parsis, who in their own smaller way stood for nonviolence and life at peace with itself. Then there is Mahatma Gandhi. In the context of the Indian ethos, the appearance of such figures is no accident. But what is that ethos? There is an answer of sorts in the ethnohistory of the subcontinent as a whole.

In 1921, an Indian archeologist, R. D. Banerji, discovered the remains of an ancient civilization at Mohenjo-daro in northern Sind. It was quickly realized that these remains were similar to those previously known, but not understood, at the site of Harappa in the Punjab. This site had been badly damaged because the bricks composing the ancient walls had been utilized for the roadbed of an Indian railroad. However, its temporal priority was recognized and the term Harappan applied to the ancient civilization. To this day, the contribution of the Harappan civilization to later Indian civilization is not clearly understood, but, as research intensifies, it is more and more taking its proper place as the foundation of that civilization.

The Harappan civilization was primarily based along the Indus River and its southern tributaries, but had settlements almost as far south as the Narbada River valley in Gujarat, as far north and east as the vicinity of Delhi, and with sites located in Makran on the west; it is regarded as one of the most areally extensive among the primary civilizations of the ancient world. Though its writing system, which is known only from seals and graffiti, is still largely undeciphered, it appears that the Harappans spoke an early language of the Dravidian family. Dravidian, now largely spoken in South India, may have a relationship to Elamite, an early language of the Iranian plateau, and possibly to other languages of inner Asia. The civilization emphasized wheat, barley, and cattle in its economy. The Harappan people were excellent metallurgists, stonecutters, and brickmakers. They appear to have organized their cities, and even the small settlements that characterized their settlement patterns, into high areas with public buildings, including granaries, and low areas for residences. They had cattle-drawn carts, played dice, provided their children with clay animal toys, some with movable heads; their women adorned themselves with multiple arm bangles and necklaces, some of which contained gold and lapis lazuli beads.

Recent research indicates that the Harappans divided their society into two great moieties. One centered around protection for the settlements, principally against animal foes, for there is little evidence to suggest alien states with which they warred. The concern seems to have been the general vulnerability of fields and flocks to the depredations of the fiercesome buffalo, rhino, and elephant who then roamed the region. The tiger, too, was obviously a threat to cattle, goat, and man. Indeed, the members of this moiety were further divided into subgroups with these fierce animals as their devices. The opposite, but paradoxically complementary, moiety was one devoted primarily to ensuring fertility. Here the domesticated animals—zebu, bull, oxen, and goat-ram—were emblematic of subgroups within the larger unit. The protective moiety was centered around a god of beasts, while the fertility half had a deity associated with the pipal or fig tree. The evidence suggests that there was a great chief over both moieties with subsidiary chiefs or head-men for each subdivision.

There appears to have been a mythic narrative in which a Herculean man destroys tigers by seizing them by the throat. He is depicted in the same fashion as the Gilgamesh figure characteristic in ancient Mesopotamian design, and is indicative of the not infre-quent contact that may have occurred between ancient India and the civilizations of the Tigris-Euphrates area, a contact not yet clear as to its motivation, commercial or other-wise. There is also a spearman who thrusts at a great water buffalo of the kind associated with the so-called Lord of Beasts described above. Another rather awesome grapheme shows this same buffalo goring long-haired women, whose dismembered bodies fly in the air. These same women appear to have been followers of the God of the Pipal Tree. Indeed, this suggests an ongoing combat between the powers of destruction and those

A group of people wash saffron flowers in Kashmir, India. Saffron, made from the stigmas of a fall-flowering crocus native to Asia Minor, is used to flavor and color food, particularly Indian food. The stigmas, which are hand picked, dried, and powdered, are deep orange, pungent, and highly valued as a spice in the West. (W. J. Morden, 1920s)

Villagers from Punjab, India, gather for a market or fair. Weekly bazaars, cattle markets,
and the larger annual religious fairs were places to buy and sell and catch up on news. (Orme, 1975)

of creation and growth. The Harappan evidence shows that the themes of protection and fertility were dominant ones in the ideology of this earliest Indian civilization. We know of processions in which effigies of certain animals, fierce and domestic, were carried on standards, and there are some depictive objects with all these animals placed in juxta-position with one another. Though our evidence is frustratingly small, it is quite obvious that the Harappans considered destruction and creation capabilities as complements rather than opposites. This is a major theme in Indian religion, and there seems little doubt that it is rooted in the ancient Harappan world view.

The Harappans' cities and towns were made to a considerable extent of fired brick. With this material they lined wells, built sewers and sumps, made bathrooms, and laid out drains. The Harappans consequently appear to have been consummate civil engineers. Two-storied houses with interior stairways, central open-air courts, stone lattice screens, and multiple service rooms were common structures, giving an aspect of wealth that may well mean that society as a whole had class divisions along lines of wealth and power. The size of the houses evidences a need for servants, and the varied fine crafts represented artifactually suggest a great number of craftsmen and other specialists, perhaps patronized by the wealthy. Populations of over twenty thousand are possible for some of the cities, but it is quite likely that the bulk of the people lived in small communities scattered over the countryside.

One of the interesting aspects of the settlements outside of the cities is that a formality of plan is revealed when they are excavated. The impression is that these small settlements were not villages but simply functional units in the midst of a spread of households. This would be something like the blockhouse settlements in early American days, when people lived by their fields and in their own widely separated houses. In times of danger they could come to the centrally located blockhouse. The Harappans, apparently, came to these central settlements not for safety, like the cities, since they are largely unwalled, though the central high place may have an enclosing wall. There is a strong suggestion that craftsmen, smiths, millers, and recorders, as well as perhaps chiefs or other authorities lived in these central sites. One can imagine a control hub where goods and services were exchanged. The households may represent all kinds of subsistence activity from simple farming to pastoralism, based on goat-sheep-cattle herding, to fishing along the shores of the Indus River or the Arabian Sea, one of the most abundantly stocked fishing grounds in the world.

The Harappans had an elaborate system of weights and measures. They appear to have estimated value, much as in the traditional bazaars of today, by weighing the product on a balance scale against a calibrated system of stone weights. (Larger weights were probably worked on a large-scale balance.) They had a calendar based on the lunar month but closely attuned to the agricultural year, which included recognition of the monsoonal months as well as the harvest and probably irrigation periods. This calendar may have been capable of delicate adjustment since it was characterized by small ivory counter sticks slid along strings on the order of the abacus.

In all this evidence there is a strong atmosphere of order and control, coupled with a keen sense of the environment and the adjustments necessary to live in it. The ancient seals have bosses at their back for the insertion of neck cords, and we can envision an elite class of seal-wearers dedicated to the well-being of the whole and administering to the needs of the larger community. Wherever archeology encounters the Harappans, essentially the same style of artifact is found. A surprising uniformity existed in Harappan settlements wherever they were located. The seals suggest that there were musicians— lyre-players and drummers; that the Harappan elite traced descent from sun, moon, and stars; that they knew five directions: east-west, up-river (north), down-river (south), and the direction of the monsoon (southwest); and that the individual seal-wearer used the name of his settlement in his proper name much as the poets of South India were to do fifteen hundred years or so later. The Harappans appear to have grown cotton, domesticated the chicken, possibly used windmills, played chess, and established settlements along major trade routes right into the interior of Asia, as far as the Oxus River. They had ships and sailed the seacoasts.

It is of value to describe Harappan accomplishment insofar as we know it, for of all the primary civilizations of the ancient world it is the least well-known. But what we do know suggests that it was far more fundamental to Indian life than even the vaunted Indo-Aryans, whose noisy place in Indian ethnohistory has often been overstated by scholars of both East and West. Controversial as this statement may be, there is no question that India's basic way of life is that of the farming village, something which undeniably owes its existence in major part to the advent and accomplishments of the

An old man sits in a doorway of a market in Ratnapura, Sri Lanka. The population of Sri Lanka increased ten times between the British occupation in 1799 and the mid twentieth century, while the land available for cultivation actually decreased. As a result, many peasants are landless and must find work in the cities. (Lee Boltin, 1955)

Snake charmers, or "snakers" as they prefer to be called, form a distinct caste in India. Snake charming is a way of life with an ethical and religious foundation, and was already present in India by the third century B.C., according to ancient sources. The poisonous snakes, mostly cobras, are rendered harmless by severing the poison ducts running to the fangs. The "charming" is actually accomplished by annoying the snake and inciting it to spread its hood. The snaker will often begin by sprinkling cold water on the snake, and he will play the flute so close to the snake that the expelled air from the flute irritates it further. (B.M. De Cou, 1924)

Harappan civilization and its generic predecessors, the early prehistoric farming and pastoral communities of the Indus River region, which lies in the strategic Indo-Iranian borderlands.

Traditionally, it is in the middle of the second millennium B.C. when in these borderlands appeared an Indo-European-speaking people referred to as the Indo-Aryans. The oral tradition known as the Veda, and more particularly the *Rig-Veda*, describes a pastoral people equipped with horse chariots, believing in essentially Central Asian gods of the sky, the storm, sun, fire, and creation, and carrying on rituals involving the consumption of an intoxicating drink called soma (probably fermented mare's milk) and the sacrifice of horses. A tradition of war chiefs and an effective priesthood provided cohesion. Pastoral nomadism, in which goats and sheep are gradually replaced by cattle, is implied and suggestive of a gradual Indianization. But it is the horse that dominates their imageries. We can detect the intoxicating joy of racing, of far journeys, and of great charges against foes. There are themes of self-sacrifice, of mighty deeds, and of heroes that are no different from those we know of Central Asian pastoralists generally.

The later Vedas and the epics, the *Mahabharata* and the *Ramayana*, which are seminal to an understanding of the traditional Indian world view, with the various commentaries and manuals of ritual such as the forest books, the *Brahmanas*, and the *Upanishads*, together form the basic literary foundation of Indian civilization. All these can be interpreted as exemplifying the sedentarization of the Indo-Aryans. There are endless statements as to the niceties of proper ritual, the meaning of this or that rite, and a remarkable play with words when the nuance is often more meaningful than the definition. The historical thread running through these texts, which after A.D. 1000 were surely increas-

An old man in Kandy, a city in Sri Lanka, carries a box and umbrella. (Lee Boltin, 1955)

Rice is piled up after drying in the sun at a rice mill in Sri Lanka. Ninety-five percent of the world's rice is produced in Asia and its offshore islands. (B. Logan, 1955)

ingly written down in an as yet unknown writing form, demonstrates the rise of urban life and the development of essentially city states from the Punjab along the Ganges-Jumna basin up to the foothills of the Himalaya.

Motivational in developing some of the most extraordinary responses in human history were the loss of the old, freer way of life; the apparent inability of the Indo-Aryan states to get along with one another; the complexities of urban life and a life increasingly based on agriculture and commerce; the ongoing challenge to traditional values; the increased rigidity and complexity of ritual and rite; and an assumed high death rate owing to the exigencies of the North Indian climate and the vectors of disease created by increasingly larger populations clustered in village and town.

In the *Mahabharata*, one of the heroes, Arjuna, caught up in internecine war that pitted relatives against relatives, friends against friends, nations against nations, ponders the fate of man on the evening before the final battle. He cannot bring himself to kill his fellow man. But his charioteer, the god Krishna, in a most moving epic song, the *Bhagavad Gita*, tells Arjuna that all men must do what they must do. It is Arjuna's duty, his dharma, to fight in the battle, and only in this way can the order of the world be maintained. Later, after the battle, the Queen Mother of the defeated, seeing the ruin of all that she has loved, cries out, Why? And like Cassandra at Troy, viewing the body of Hector, she speaks of the anguish of all mankind.

In the Indo-Aryan kingdom of Sakya, in the foothills of the Himalaya, a king tries to keep his son and heir from the ugliness of the world. He creates great pleasure gardens and surrounds the young prince with all that is desirable, all that can give material happiness. But the prince is witness to human suffering in various forms and, seeing an ascetic, he at last renounces the throne and wanders across India as an ascetic himself. After many years he can go no farther in his search for he realizes that not through wandering will enlightenment come but through a struggle within himself. He resolves to take up that struggle and under the bodhi tree ponders the circumstances of life and death,

Indians gather at a well near Fatephur Sikri, Uttar Pradesh, India. Women and children often carry water from distant wells to their homes. Round-bottomed water pots, traditionally made of pottery or brass, are today also made of aluminum and plastic. (B.M. De Cou, 1924)

and the essential mortality of all living things caught in an eternal cycle of birth and rebirth. His answer is simple. It comes literally with a bowl of milk proferred to him by a little girl who pities his lonely vigil. It is known as the Four Noble Truths: suffering exists; suffering is caused by desire; suffering can be overcome by the elimination of desire; desire can be eliminated by following the *Noble Eightfold Path*. The *Eightfold Path* is essentially a formula of moderation and clear thought, actually a statement of the role of reason in human affairs. The prince now is known as the Buddha, the Enlightened One, who, until his death at the age of eighty, preached to all who would listen to the application of his truths to daily life. After his death Buddhism took many forms, some of which will be described later. But at its heart Buddhism addresses itself marvelously to the human condition. For example, the emperor Asoka (whose pillar capital graces the flag of modern India), one of the most powerful monarchs in Indian history, renounced warfare completely after seeing the slaughter caused by his armies in Orissa. His concern for life was so great that he even restricted the killing of animals. His decrees for actively waging peace were set up on the bounds of his empire from southern Afghanistan to Bengal, Orissa, and far into South India.

The great teacher Mahavira, who was a contemporary of the Buddha, taught that all things have souls and these souls are locked into substance. All souls feel pain when their substance is hurt. Thus a tree being chopped, an insect flying into one's eye, the ant stepped on in the road, all feel pain and cry out in their own way, just as man does in similar circumstances. The point of life is to avoid giving pain so that one's own soul may perhaps be unblemished and some hope of escape from substance be obtained. Jain monks walk about with their mouths cloth-covered and carrying fly whisks to avoid injury to insects. The Jains have a fine hospital for hurt pigeons in Delhi. Jains do not kick stones for fear of hurting the soul within. Kindliness and charity are daily requirements of Jain action.

Tea is an important crop in Bangladesh, where thousands of acres are under cultivation. Here, Hindu teapickers are returning to the fields. (Jean and Franc Shor, recent)

Villagers relax in a settlement in Lucknow district. Their homes consist of simple mud-plastered huts with thatched roofs. Every village in India has an open area where people of the same caste can rest, relax, or hold civic functions. (A.S. Vernay, 1920s)

A common sight in India is the drying of dung for use as fuel. Sometimes pats are slapped against the sides of houses or laid out in elaborate patterns in the sun. India has one of the largest livestock populations of any country in the world—a steady source of fuel. (Orme, recent)

Hinduism, which steadily grew as the most important faith in India from a century or two before the time of Christ, also contains marvelously balanced views as to the responsibility of individual man for his own actions. The basic theme found in both Buddhism and Hinduism is the concept of rebirths. All living things are part of a perpetual cycle of existence. Like the second law of thermodynamics, nothing is lost in whatever form it happens to be. There is in Hinduism a basic reality: man is responsible for his own actions and must fulfill the ends of life whatever his circumstances in any particular rebirth. Remarkable in their acknowledgment of human nature, these four ends are the pursuit of pleasure, kama; the seeking of material gain, artha; the restraint necessary to do one's duty in life correctly, dharma; the eventual renunciation of the other three in order to be freed from worldliness through a religious objective, moksha. For each of these ends much was written. Of them all, dharma was and is the most important since its emphasis on duty, justice, and rightness affects performance within the other three. This is a major theme in both the *Mahabharata* and the *Ramayana*. The latter epic is concerned with the abduction of Sita, the wife of Prince Rama, by the demonic king Ravana, who takes her to Ceylon. After numerous adventures, Rama, with the effective aid of his brother and the Monkey King Hanuman, rescues Sita. The story is replete with the lures and temptations of life and the responses the heroes give to them, responses ultimately made possible by virtue or dharma.

But the ancient Indian was much concerned with the proper way to manifest all the ends of man. The famous *Kamasutra* of Vatsyayana describes the proper way to pursue pleasure. The sage Bharata wrote a treatise on the dramatic arts, the *Natyasastra*, which elucidates the methods of artistic expression of the emotions and is the basis of traditional Indian dance-theater. Kautilya, a prime minister to Chandragupta Maurya, wrote the *Arthasastra*, which is a treatise on the practice of government comparable to Machiavelli's *The Prince* in its comment on the acquisition and uses of power by the sovereign, while the Lawbook of Manu reasserts the ideals of the earlier Brahmanic faith within the state.

The *Bhagavad Gita* is to many the supreme statement of Indian ideas as to the place of man in the cosmos. It addresses itself to moksha, the fourth end of man. At heart, it emphasizes the individual's personal relationship to divinity, the consequence of which is to bring that divinity into one's own actions, enabling one to fulfill his obligations to society in the fullest way possible. But a critical idea is that those obligations may involve self-sacrifice; indeed, the point of fulfilling one's duty is not to obtain secular advantage or other material gain for oneself, but to act for the good of society. There is a wonderful modern example of this idea of individual renunciation for society's sake in Shri Lal Bahadur Shastri's life. As successor to the prime ministership of India after Jawaharlal Nehru's death, Shastri was the most powerful figure in India. He died suddenly in Tashkent during the successful negotiations for a peace between India and Pakistan. When his total worldly estate was calculated, his wealth was about ten dollars! So devoted had he been to his role as a servant of the people that he had renounced all opportunity to profit!

The *Bhagavad Gita* is concerned with the sayings of Lord Krishna, one of the most popular gods in India. Anyone superficially studying Hinduism is immediately struck by the multiplicity of deities present. Historically, it appears that much of that multiplicity was caused by amalgams between the pantheistic Vedic tradition and local beliefs of tribal India. However, the now classical grouping of these gods has three main themes: creation (Brahma), destruction (Siva), and preservation (Vishnu). Paradoxically, each of

Kashmir is renowned for its high-quality woolen cloth and "cashmere" shawls, which a weaver is making here. Notice the intricate design that requires many bobbins. (W. J. Morden, 1920s)

127

these powers also contains its opposite. That is, Siva's destruction is also an act of preservation; with Vishnu's preservation is involved the act of destruction; and the implication of Brahma's creation is, of course, noncreation. Evidences for these divine paradoxes are found in Hindu mythology. Siva, for example, has consorts that are benign in appearance and action, but have savage demonic aspects. Vishnu is as capable of bringing fire and flood as he is of playing the flute for the dances of shepherdesses in some wooded glade. Vishnu's varied selves, or avatars, include Rama and Krishna among many others and attest to the multifaceted character of that deity.

All of Hinduism's gods and goddesses require rites, festivals, and other devotional acts. This is in keeping with the idea of sublimating individual identity to the larger divine. The celebrated devotional yoga (bhakti yoga), in which an essential element is meditation on oneness, whatever it may be, brings the individual into a direct relationship to divinity, whatever that may be. Esoteric Hinduism considers self to be mere illusion in the context of the ultimate oneness or universal self. To a very real extent every deity in the great tradition of Hinduism is like a key on a large cosmic instrument: each gives forth a particular sound, a resonance if you will, which is a special sonant in an ultimate music of the spheres. The myths and legends gathered around these deities are the basis of favorite narrative embellishments, which are understandable to every villager from Cape Comorin to the slopes of the Himalaya.

In earlier times, by far the largest number of Indians lived in villages, tilling the soil of their forefathers, hoping for the monsoon rains to come in the terribly hot spring, and hoping they will abate at crucial times in the humid summer. The village was dominated by a work ethic in which social recognition was gained by labor and the ability to fulfill one's role in the larger village society. Villages varied in plan and economic emphasis all over India. The Bengalis and Tamils were rice growers; the Punjabi grew wheat; all tried to raise garden crops of chilis, tomatoes, and other vegetables. Practically all village farms used bullocks for plowing and hauling. Cattle were respected for their divine connections, and meat eating was a rarity partly because meat animals were difficult to raise and partly because meat eating was generally regarded as impure.

Most villages have a tank, or small open body of water, near the village temple or shrine. Trees are kept for shade and fruit. The Indian house is a shelter during the rains, but most village life takes place outside, on the porches, in the yards and open spaces where cooking, eating, and socializing occur. Charpoys, hammocks, and bench beds are for sleeping in a special room or on a roof. Earlier, the houses were mostly of mud and clay, made either into brick or adobe, or plastered over a screen of branches. Straw roofs are favorite places for rats and their predators, the rat snake; gekkos and a multitude of varied birds consume the abundant insect life. Festivals are numerous and color the otherwise drab work year with processions, competitions, rites, theater troupes, and feasts on a

(text continued on page 141)

In this brass oil lamp from India the oil filled the animal's body while the wick emerged from the top of the bird head. The juxtaposition of bird and animal forms is interesting; however, it is possible that the two pieces came from different lamps. Height: 6 inches

Around 2000 B.C. a group of people from Central Asia invaded and settled India.
Called the Indo-Aryans, these people worshiped gods of the storm and fire and
sacrificed horses. In some villages in India today, craftsmen make clay horses that are
ritually broken at certain times of the year, reminiscent of the ancient Aryan custom.
Height: (left) 20 inches; (right) 12 inches

OPPOSITE:

This goat is made of zinc-copper alloy that was cast in a mold and blackened. Designs
are cut in intaglio and the spaces inlayed with silver and brass. The technique
originated in the Middle East and is commonly called Damascene Ware. It was
practiced in various centers in India by Muslim craftsmen. Height: 9¾ inches

As the auspicious goddess of good fortune and abundance, Gaja Lakshmi is often placed over a doorway. This perforated wooden panel from South India (c. nineteenth century) would most likely have been used in this position. Gaja Lakshmi, wife of Vishnu, is always shown being anointed with water by a pair of elephants. Height: 10¾ inches

OPPOSITE:

Originally part of a ritual temple chariot from South India, this carved and painted eighteenth-century wooden horse is one of a pair. These chariots provided transportation for temple deities during annual festivals. Height: 83 inches

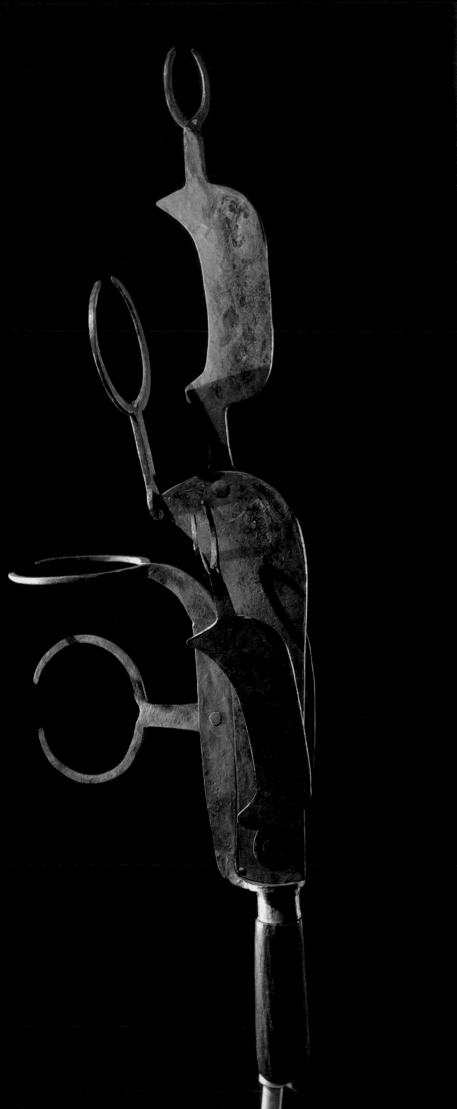

Elaborate iron and wood funeral knives, called urkatti, *were displayed only at funerals of important old men of the Badaga tribe, which dwells in the Nilgiri Hills, South India. This grotesque instrument, which is very rare, was intended to ward off evil spirits that might be hovering over the funeral procession. Half of a lime was usually speared on one blade so the juice would sting the spirit's eyes. Height: 25 inches*

OPPOSITE:

Ritual oil lamps, deepas, *are used in worship throughout India. This finial to a free-standing South Indian brass oil lamp is in the form of a* hamsa *or gander with vegetation coming out of its mouth. Height: 27 inches*

The wife of Siva the Destroyer takes many forms. Here she is Kali, a particularly ferocious representation, depicted in bronze from South India; c. 1800. Height: 9½ inches

Ganesha, the elephant-headed son of Siva, is the Hindu god of wisdom. As the placer and remover of obstacles, his blessing is invoked at the beginning of all undertakings. This bronze image from South India dates from the seventeenth century. Height: 13 inches

Indian village craftsmen work with brass in many different techniques. The two peacocks from Bihar are fine examples of the lost-wax process. Strands of wax placed over a clay core are melted away and replaced by brass during the casting process. The fish from Orissa is constructed of overlapping brass segments for movement. Both are from the twentieth century. Height: (peacock, left) 12 inches; (right) 15¼ inches. Length: (fish) 17½ inches

(text continued from page 128)

larger or smaller scale, depending on tradition and on the economic and social commitments involved.

Essential to the individual's identity is that he be recognized by as large a group as possible. This recognition gives him the social status vital to inner well-being. For in spite of the seeming paradox of individual moksha and social recognition, there is no real contradiction. Only when one has related fruitfully to society through action is there a reason for self-effacement before the divine. From birth to death, identity in the larger society beyond the family is a constant need. Friendships, marriage relations, economic ties, political alliances, victories in competition, special talents, all have their role and are all viable means of obtaining wider recognition. What is, however, vital to this recognition is that it must be in the context of village harmony, not disruption. At babyhood, the disruptive child is isolated from the food games of the others and receives no effective response to his complaining; the quarrel between husband and wife is the object of local gossip and both lose face; the son who does not help his father loses recognition by the village elders; and the village thief does not need to be found guilty by a regularly constituted court for he is ostracized and literally compelled to leave. In other words, shame and loss of face act in counterbalance to the possibilities of overstatement or negative recognition in village life.

Traditionally, marriage has been arranged by a go-between who tries to obtain advantages for her employer in terms of social status and economic return. As in so much of Asia, marriage involves an economic and social exchange of value for both families. This often means that affairs of the heart are subordinate to the requirements of material status. In this regard the position of Indian women is related to inheritance, which tends to go from father to deserving son; male authority in most village affairs is a matter of custom. But in actual fact, the typical Indian village farming family is a work unit in which men and women labor side by side at harvest and seeding time, or complement one another at other times of the year. Familial decisions tend to be bilateral, as they are in the West, and are based on the practicalities of daily life; in this aspect Hindu village women tend to be far less bound by custom than their counterparts in either traditional China or the Near East. Older customs, such as child marriage and widow isolation, where a second marriage was impossible even though the girl had been pledged to a boy in preadolescent years, have been vanishing gradually from the Indian scene. There still remain the perennial problems of high child mortality and lack of birth control, which the government of India struggles to help her people overcome.

"Indian society is divided into castes or *jatis*." This statement, found in hundreds of books dealing with Indian life, is a fact, but Westerners often understand it as something of a fiction. *Jati*, as we shall call it here, can be regarded in its best sense as a functioning

This door guardian, or dvarapala, *is one of a pair. His characteristic bulging eyes and ferocious expression along with the snake and drum, imply that he once guarded a temple dedicated to Siva. From South India, this eighteenth-century carved wooden figure is covered with gessoed and painted cloth. Height: 93 inches*

Andamese greetings and departures are
emotional affairs. This rather didactic
photograph shows greetings (right), where the
two people sit weeping with arms encircling
each other. When parting (left), the one who
is leaving takes his friend's hand and blows
on it. (C. Anderson, 1908)

The Andaman Islands, a small chain in the
Bay of Bengal, are inhabited by people who
are one of the few negroid populations of Asia.
Ptolemy is believed to have referred to the
Andamese when he described the
Anthropophagi "whose heads grow beneath
their shoulders." An Andamese custom is to
wear the skulls of deceased relatives suspended
from the neck. This man is shooting fish with
a bow of chai wood and slender bamboo arrows
tipped with iron. (C. Anderson, 1908)

part of the large organism that is Indian society. A person is born into a *jati* and can never leave it. To it, he has a particular obligation. Since most Indian *jatis* are occupational units, one's obvious duty is to fulfill that occupation in the best way possible. *Jati* occupations cover the whole gamut of goods and service relationships, and each *jati* is thus in symbiosis with all the others. Whether it be the Brahman priest at the top, or the untouchable at the bottom, there is an obligation to do what has to be done according to the perimeters of the *jati*. While *jatis* are occupationally divided, it is this symbiotic relationship that binds them together, plus commonalities of language, village residence, and historical tradition. Each *jati* has its own rituals, values, habits of dressing and eating, and ways of thinking about the world. In terms of religion, the habits of eating grade the *jati* according to levels of purity, with the purest being the Brahman *jati*, solely vegetarian, and the lowest tending to be those who eat meat.

The origins of *jati* are not clear. It is apparent that *jatis* have multiplied greatly in number in the last three hundred years, mostly in response to the changes caused by contacts with Western invention or by contacts brought about by improving communications with the larger India. This does not, of course, explain the *jati's* origins, but it does point up the fact that the *jati* system, far from being frozen into rigidity, retains a flexibility so that it responds as challenges are brought to it by a changing world. For example, a *jati* of leatherworkers may divide on the basis of different needs for leather—from the shoemaker to the bookbinder—each eventually forming a different *jati*, which in turn develops its own laws and values.

What is so fascinating about *jati* is that it has the effect of interrelating villages over the entire Indian landscape. Not all villages have all *jatis*, of course, and since *jati* endogamy must be practiced, the choice of a marriage partner in most villages must be made outside of the resident village. Thus, where *jati* is practiced, the village *jatis* are vertically arranged, but the individuals making up each *jati* are occupationally and even politically related across *jati* in the village structure. By marriage and by specialization, however, the individual is also related to his own *jati* as it is found in other villages, perhaps miles away. We thus have village exogamy and *jati* endogamy. This has the effect of giving the individual two social positions at birth: one in the vertical structure of his own village, and one in villages where his *jati* is also located.

In these ways India's villages relate to one another not only in the natural course of common concern about the redistribution of market crops, and the goods and services function of local and regional authority, but in the natural social requirements of the life cycle. For all *jati* interrelationships across villages are a vital part of establishing individual identity. Anthropologists have called the Indian village a node in a vast network which covers all India and gives to all a place in time and space.

There is, however, another important element in Indian life: the Indian villager's life is made cohesive by a teeming body of local traditions, which include local deities unrecognized in the classic Hindu pantheon; local saints, witches, superstitions; ways of building houses; styles of color and form in dress; art, music, folk tales, and dialectal manners, in fact, a multitude of indigenous ways adding up to a dynamic folk order. The visitor to India can recognize aspects of this element in Indian life by carefully scrutinizing costume, folk art, jewelry, and music. These are surface indications of the vast variety of local beliefs, styles, and values that anthropologists call the "Little Tradition."

In contrast, in the "Great Tradition" are the overriding elements of Indian culture, such as the Sanskrit language; the classical Hindu deities and certain of the festivals such as Holi and Divalia, the Festival of Lights; and the government of India. Obviously, "Great Tradition" ideas and manifestations are more apparent in India's cities and towns than in the villages. Yet the "Great Tradition" is everywhere and has been since the time of Asoka (reigned c. 269–232 B.C.) and perhaps before. In India, these two traditions have merged. This integration is not one-sided, for many of the apparent universals of Indian life are the consequence of village traditions.

These are some of India's responses to the complexity of life that concerned the heroes of the *Mahabharata*, and that motivated the Buddha and his countryman Mahavira long ago. It is no coincidence that Mahatma Gandhi turned to India's village life as the ideal for the whole state. He himself dressed in the simple dhoti (loincloth) of village India and wore plain cloth in the fine city hotels as a constant reminder of that heritage.

But so much of Indian history is recounted in terms of North India where the foreigner continually set his foot. South India, however, was never completely conquered until the British came with their ships. Village life had come there around a thousand years before Christ and had expanded into a civilized life with the development of fine cities and towns primarily for trade and royal administration. The Tamil poetic anthologies describe princes, princesses, merchants, bards, soldiers, musicians, and all the specialized activities common to civilization. By a few centuries before Christ these flourishing centers of South India were motivating some of the finest poets in Asian history to write dazzling human lyrics of love and sadness, joy and loneliness. It was a time that in its own way is comparable to the golden ages of literature celebrated in Europe and it is only now coming into its own in the West. Here is a short poem by one of the greatest of the classical Tamil poets, Kapila (sixth century B.C.). It must stand for them all:

> *What He Said*
> *My love is a two-faced thief.*
> *In the dead of night*
> *she comes like the fragrance*
> *of the Red-speared Chieftain's forest hills,*
> *to be one with me.*
>
> *And then, she sheds the petals*
> *of night's several flowers,*
> *and does her hair again*
> *with new perfumes and oils,*
> *to be one with her family at dawn*
>
> *With a stranger's different face.*
>
> (THE INTERIOR LANDSCAPE, translated by A. K. Ramanujan. Bloomington, Indiana University Press, p. 92.)

A woman carries a heavy load in Darjeeling, an Indian town in the Himalayan foothills. (B.M. De Cou, 1924)

These performers are dressed for a dance-drama, an ancient tradition of India. Troupes of actors, dancers, and musicians, usually male, toured the countryside performing dance-dramas based on religious and mythical themes. These troupes were very popular, and enthralled audiences would sometimes sit through the night watching a performance. (A.S. Vernay, 1920s)

The Muslim conquest of North India, which began with the Arab conquest of Sind in the eighth century and was crowned by the Empire of the Mughals beginning in the sixteenth century, struck a powerful blow at the native traditions. But with a tenacity that still marks India today, much of the tradition survived. Yet the Muslim-Hindu confrontation has never been marked by long periods of peace. Both Mahmud of Ghazni and Tamerlane slaughtered Hindus and piled their skulls in pyramids outside Delhi, while anti-Hindu policies of many Muslim governments left a great crevice between different peoples that divides India and the Muslim state of Pakistan even today. Yet there were times when this enmity hardly existed. For the Muslim rulers in India had to accept the fact that ruling successfully meant ruling with justice—not simply justice for Muslims and injustice for Hindus, but justice for all. Some made valiant efforts to do just that, the most notable being the great Mughal ruler Akbar, a contemporary of Queen Elizabeth I of England, who, deeply religious himself, listened to proponents of many faiths, including Christianity. His policy of tolerance led to greater harmony than had ever before been found in the Muslim state generally. He left an enduring monument by demonstrating that given understanding and legal rights Hindu and Muslim could get along harmoniously.

The Mughals left other monuments of which the Taj Mahal is the most famous. Although based on Persian design, the Taj has become one of India's most famous symbols. It is as if the Mughal emperor Jahan had built the Taj Mahal not so much as a tomb for his beloved, but rather to provide something beautiful in homage to the Hindustan over which he reigned. That same sense is felt in the history of British India, for when regarding the accomplishments of that empire in India one finds that many British officials, realizing that British control could not last forever, wanted to leave an India that would be a monument to their justice and understanding. As one British official said, "India brings out the best in a man or it can bring out the worst, but if the latter it was there already, if the former it was India that put it there in the first place, and it is our job to use it well so when we leave they can say 'well done'."

The widespread influence of Indian culture is a testimony to the accomplishments of that enduring civilization. It is no coincidence that one part of Southeast Asia has been called Indo-China, or that Sri Lanka has an important place in the *Ramayana*, or that a number of sects of Tibetan Buddhism acknowledge India as their founders. Yet beyond these obvious contributions India is a testimony to the capability of a special kind of civilization to endure. The almost incredible variety of ways of life, languages, and cultures that we symbolize when we say the name "India" seems almost paradoxical. That very unity in diversity has endured because it rests on the secure foundation that where there is knowledge all things have their place, and that India's supreme wise men have championed peace more than any other civilization in human history.

When the Sikh father spanks his child for naughtiness, he ends by clutching the child to him and commiserating. By this act he is saying, "Whatever you've done, whatever the consequence, I'm with you, my child." Many believe that whatever happens to the world, India will remain to lead men back to sanity. As Gandhi said, "It is India's dharma to do so."

THE CHINESE YIN-YANG

CHINA IS A LAND OF VIVID CONTRASTS: the endless brown-green countryside with the drab appearance of working people in contrast to the brilliant colors of street processions and the interior walls of temples and halls; the enormous masses of people, who have literally consumed the countryside, and the solitary figure of a sage amid flourishing trees and pristine cloud-suggested mountains of Taoist painting; the calmness of an old man's bearded face emanating the wisdom of maturity and the singsong wail of the actor in the Peking Opera; the clack-clack of the street vendor's wooden cymbals in the early morning and the perpetual hubbub of the incredibly crowded streets. The smells of China are the weighted odors of night soil, fish, and jasmine as opposed to the feather aromas of fine tea, dark timber, and sandalwood. Thoughts in China are simplistic, pragmatic, cause-and-effect peasant ones; they mark village and collective-state affairs, and the sequenceless dualism in unity that is incomprehensible to the mathematically minded materialists of the West.

Above all, there is the land, China's measure of value, for what produces causes food, and what does not produce causes famine. It is that simple. There is no escaping from that equation in a land where the world's largest population is concentrated. Those who want to understand China must start with the Chinese farmer, his land, and the social fact that large family cohesiveness was both an economic and ideological virtue. The Chinese thus concentrated wherever soil and water allowed it, rather than fanning out in small households over the landscape. Even in Confucius's day (sixth–fifth century B.C.), when the population was not a twentieth of what it is now, the small China of the northeast was crowded as families stayed together for centuries in one or two places. With a technology of hand tools, and animal- or human-drawn plows and carts, every member of the family had a role—brothers, fathers, sons for breaking the soil, sisters, daughters, wives for seeding and harvest. It is no wonder that every effort was made to keep the large, extended family together.

Directly related to this man-land intimacy was the contempt that the Chinese have had for the merchant and soldier. Neither of these occupations results in foodstuff or the permanency of family. The merchant is a nonproducer seeking his own profit. The soldier has uses, but if he is killed far away he cannot observe filial piety. Nothing shows China's change more than the expansion of standing armies and the creation of a military elite.

Emphasis on man marks Chinese thought not only in the Classic Age but in modern times. What was critical was to bring order out of disorder. In general, the way shared by almost all Chinese thinkers from Confucius to Mao Tse-tung was to combine study of a situation with the hard work of rectifying it. The enormous sense of men's dependence upon one another stands out. The great Taoist philosopher Chuang-Tzu (fourth–third century B.C.), who in his hermitlike existence conceived of man and man's actions as artificial in the context of nature, still saw life as a series of dependencies before which man was to live in moderation. A shadow was once asked, "At one moment you move; at another you are at rest. At one moment you sit down; at another you stand up. Why are you so inconsistent?" The shadow answered, "Do I not have to depend upon something else for doing what I do? Does not that something upon which I depend still have to depend upon something else for doing what it does?"

Hand-puppet theater is an ancient tradition in China and is still widely practiced today. The popular puppet theater dramatizes stories, legends, myth, and history in a lively and often humorous way. The puppeteers are extraordinarily dextrous and can make their puppets tumble, leap, smoke real pipes, drink tea, fight with swords, and take their coats on and off. The puppets themselves are carved in camphor wood, lacquered, and dressed in exquisitely embroidered silks. In keeping with Chinese tradition, their heads are removed between performances to prevent them from coming to life. (1917)

China's social, cultural, and economic structure traditionally rested on agriculture. Land was intensively and efficiently farmed; this scene shows two farmers irrigating a field with an irrigation wheel.

This relativity of action in the midst of nature acts as a measure for men to comprehend the world. To the Confucian, the measurement is against the standards of the sages and kings of antiquity as set forth in the classic Books of Odes, Rites, History, and Music, the Spring and Autumn Annals, and the Book of Changes; to the Taoist, it is nature itself manifest apparently as a duality, Yin-Yang, but actually a unity comprehensible only as experience. To the Chinese farmer, the measurement is a relationship between work and result.

But these relationships did not always bear fruit. During a crisis in the state, advisors to the monarch sometimes advised him to destroy the Confucian grasp upon affairs. In the Ch'in dynasty (255–206 B.C.), there was even a burning of books and a massacre of scholars. Some advisors to the last emperors of China in the nineteenth century deplored the Confucian role in determining China's future. For the bureaucrats obtained their position by passing examinations in the Confucian classics! Taoism had a tendency to cause men to withdraw from the world and by so doing underlined a fundamental selfishness in which self-identity in nature might be more important than humanity's lot. The Chinese farmer found that flood, locust, drought, banditry, and exploitation took from his living no matter how hard he worked. There was great difficulty in sustaining the theory in the face of practice, as recorded in human history.

China's civilization arose in North China in the second millennium B.C. as a consequence of several thousand years of prehistoric development. The site of Pan-P'o, in Shensi province, represents a village already dependent on cereal agriculture and domestic animals such as the pig. The people may have painted their faces as well as their handsome pottery. They appear to have believed in some form of afterlife since their cemeteries contain funerary furniture, including useful tools. Their houses were round or squarish, semisubterranean, and apparently thatched as in the modern style. What stands out is the clustering of houses and the careful placement of settlements near a river and in the midst of fertile soil. From these old village settlements arose more elaborate developments that included what may have been market towns in a network of villages.

North China is a broad alluvial plain. Even with the mighty Yellow River in its midst, however, agricultural settlements on that plain were not like those of the Nile, Tigris-Euphrates, or Indus river valleys. For these rivers flow through generally rainless country, limiting agricultural activity to the river vicinity, however extended through irrigation. In contrast, North China has a yearly rainfall of more than twenty inches, with most of it falling in the summer months. This enables the Chinese to cultivate intensively the soil in the rainfall period and allows for the wide dispersion of settlements.

The evidence is that the early farmers practiced a slash-and-burn agriculture, moving about according to the duration of fertility in any given area. Perhaps they were the first to clear the forest from the North China plain. This dispersion in prehistoric times may have been a factor in helping to create centers between communities for exchanging goods and sharing information. But there are other reasons.

Characteristic of Chinese families is the practice of exogamy, and the seeking of women in other settlements than their own may well have been part of prehistoric village farm communities. Thus, kinship ties from village to village, as well as economic ones, probably existed. Since these early villages shared so much artifactually, it is also likely that they shared ideologically. As the settlements grew in size, there were probably some among them that had particular roles in religious activities, as shown by excavated remains.

The Chinese have a rich mythology which has many concepts of creation and of how the world is classified. Most of these myths are later in origin, but there is a suggestion of primeval ideas of sacrifice and of the duality of things: the world began as the consequence of the division of a cosmic egg; mountains are sacred; the sky is round; the earth is square; tortoises are supporters of structures; the cardinal directions are symbolized by animals—a red bird for the south, a tiger for the west, a tortoise and/or snake for the north, a dragon for the east. The idea that the earth is square in shape, surrounded by seas, had a particular meaning for the ancient Chinese. The notion of squares within or upon squares gives a perfectly understandable vision of world order: the sun can be conceived of as a square surmounting all other squares; and there is much evidence for the square as the basic shape of ancient Chinese cities, within which square structures, mounds, and monuments could be found.

How much these mythological concepts owed to prehistoric China is not known, but the appearance of China's first historically authenticated dynasty, the Shang (c. 1766–1122 B.C.), shows their longevity. The Shang capital, modern Anyang, has been found, and, in spite of the vicissitudes China has had to face since the site's discovery in 1927, much has been learned archeologically from this and other Shang sites of North China. What is known is that the Shang leaders formed an aristocracy ruling over a society divided into a

A Chinese fisherman with his cormorants floats on the Yangtze River near Tungchwo. The cormorants, which wore rings around their necks, could catch fish but not swallow them. (Roy Chapman Andrews, 1921)

The Chinese used a number of ingenious techniques to fish. The large net shown here was lowered by pulleys and winches into the water and then raised, capturing any fish that happened to be passing over the net. Sometimes the fisherman would smear egg whites on the net to attract fish. The smaller, long-handled net was used to remove fish from the dip net.

This is the old Summer Palace, called Pi-sha Shan-chang, or "Mountain Village for Escaping from the Heat," used as a retreat by the Manchu emperors until 1820. In this area there was also a very large tract of land reserved as an imperial hunting ground, but during the nineteenth century more and more squatters moved in. (probably early 20th century)

Travelers stop on a road in Yunnan, China. Ponies were commonly used for transport, and the trident was a weapon used against bandits or tigers. (Roy Chapman Andrews, 1916)

highly organized body of specialists—priests, metallurgists, potters, jewelers, jade-carvers, and so on. Farmers were tightly woven into the society since their villages were part of the settlement group with the administrative and ideological center in its midst. Slave labor may have been responsible for the construction of great wall- and moat-enclosed cities and for the enormous tombs complete with chariots, bronze vessels, weapons, and sacrificed horses, dogs, and men by the dozen, in which were buried Shang kings. The bronzes, decorated with fantastic designs, including the t'ao-t'ieh mask, are among the world's great art treasures. But more important, perhaps, is the fact that writing makes its appearance among these remains. It is found largely on cow-bone scapulae and on turtle shells. A question was asked by writing on the bone and the answer was obtained by heating a part of the bone, the resulting cracks being "read" as the answer. This oracular quality has given this early writing the label of "oracle writing."

Chinese writing is ideographic, that is, each sign stands for a word. The signs in Shang times were basically stylized pictures (about 2,500 of them). The Chinese characters of later times are frequently these same pictures altered by using the brush and by symbolic needs that suggest rather than depict. To write Chinese means to conceive of meaning and to select the right characters for that meaning, not on the basis of their sound values, but for semantic reasons. When one considers that the Chinese can have a hundred words meaning justice, the dozen or so possibilities in English seem limiting indeed. In the People's Republic of China, the emphasis is both on reducing the number of written characters in daily use and on simplifying their construction. New vocabularies tend to be scientific and nonhumanistic—a trend that may well mark the future as surely as Shang oracle writing marked the past.

The American Museum made extensive fossil collections in China; this view looks down from Dragon Bone Ridge, where the Central Asiatic Expedition spent weeks digging up fossils. The elaborate terracing of rice paddies is typical of the hilly regions of Szechuan, China. The building in the foreground is the T'an ancestral hall, where members of the expedition stayed. (W. Granger, 1921–22)

153

Chinese inns (at right) and store fronts were opened by removing wood shutters during the day, and closed up at night; goods were not usually displayed on the street. Most city buildings were two or three stories, roofed with tile. Drying sweet potato vines hang from the rafters of the inn. (W. Granger, 1922–23)

After the Shang dynasty came the Chou dynasty (c. 1122–221 B.C.), the Classic Age. What is obvious in the *total* Shang-Chou age is the growing emphasis on man, who, no matter how affected by superstition, deity, the events of history, or the vagaries of nature, is in the end the true link between the real world of the senses and that of the cosmos, however conceived. Asked about ghosts and spirits, Confucius said, "We don't know yet how to serve men, how can we know about serving the spirits?" Asked about death, Confucius said, "We don't know yet about life, how can we know about death?"

The sage K'ung Fu-tzu, known to the West as Confucius (c. 551–c. 479 B.C.), lived in a time of great trouble for China. It was the latter part of a period often referred to as the Classic Age because of the many writings important to the Chinese tradition that were composed or compiled by famous men. Confucius appears to have been a thoughtful, observant youth increasingly troubled by the civil wars and by other problems at a time when the central authority was no longer strong enough to control the warring barons. Basic to Confucius's thinking was the idea that in the early part of the Classic Age peace and prosperity had been brought about by ideal rulers who modeled their authority on the natural harmonies of the world. In other words, to bring order out of disorder the people of China had to look back to the time when there had been order. Confucius obtained the books of rites and rituals used by the early rulers and brought them to the people. He insisted that the ancient rites be observed to the letter, thus imbuing his ideal model with a living reality. And since the ruler was expected to keep the ideals of the past before him, he had to act morally to his subjects. His greatest obligation to the people was to gain their confidence, which necessitated keeping their needs steadily in mind, just as a father must keep his family in mind if it is to flourish.

This familial relationship is basic to the Confucian ideal. The search for natural laws on which to base state authority and the order of life that characterized the European Enlightenment, climaxing with the concept of individual freedom, came about some twenty-two hundred years after the time of Confucius, a time in China when many Chinese were seeking answers to the problems of living. Among them were Lao Tzu (born c. 604 B.C.), the proverbial founder of Taoism, and Mo Tzu (c. 470–391 B.C.), the utilitarian who made the benefits obtained by working for the future paramount. Confucius himself had numerous important followers, including Hsun Tzu and Mencius. Confucianism flourished increasingly over other world concepts with such men to implement it.

Streets in most Chinese cities are narrow, rarely exceeding twelve feet in width. Bamboo scaffolding, visible in this scene of a Hong Kong street, prevented building facades from collapsing during minor tremors. (B.M. De Cou, 1924)

Confucianism became central to Chinese life not simply because of great philosophical champions, but because of the obvious fact that the family in any individual's life has, or ought to have, a central place. When familial relationships are extended into society and sustained by the same qualities that make them vital to familial harmony, then the state, of which that society is a part, will be harmonious and a natural order will control human affairs. The Confucian system, therefore, discerns five basic relationships. Three are familial: father to son, husband to wife, older brother to younger brother. One is social: friend to friend. One relates to the state: ruler to subject. These relationships depend ultimately upon mutual respect, but it is a respect that can come only from the self-cultivation of virtue. The emphasis for those who ruled had to be on education. In this, Confucius had a sure instinct about human character. "By nature men are very much alike; it is learning and the practice of learning that sets them apart."

An essential ingredient of the familial relationships is filial piety. This refers to the respect of children not only for their living parents but for the dead as well. The traditional Chinese concept of self can be depicted as a familial chain stretching between the remote past and the near future. The individual is one link on the chain. He owes his being to the past and is thus responsible for assuring a future for his family line. Since the Chinese family is patrilineal, sons must marry and produce male offspring so that the family name and property may be perpetuated. This is a primary element in filial piety. A son's most unfilial act is not to produce sons, for that endangers the perpetuation of the family name and thus denies respect for the ancestors.

The ideal Chinese household, according to the Confucian ethic, is one in which many sons live together with their wives and children under the same roof. It is said that long ago there was a family where some two hundred members lived together. So rare was this, that the emperor himself called the grandfather to his court and asked him how he managed to keep harmony in so large a group. The old man's smiling answer was repeated numerous times: "Patience, patience, patience."

In point of fact, there was great difficulty in keeping married sons together. But whatever happened, they still observed filial piety to the founding ancestor of the family and brought up their children within the familial tradition. From this practice of perpetuating the family name, even when far from the place of familial origin, springs an important element of Chinese life—ancestor worship.

The peasants worship their ancestors as though they are spirits; with others, it is more a ritualized way of honoring one's predecessors. It involves rites of incense burning, prayer, and offerings, which can be a daily event in some homes or be observed on certain days during the year. There is usually a place in the home with an altar. Here are placed wooden tablets on which the ancestral names are written and before which the rites are performed. Characteristic of communities where numerous related families re-

(text continued on page 169)

Although brilliantly colored monochrome glazes first gained acceptance in the K'ang-hsi period, they remained popular throughout the Ch'ing period, as this example, probably from the nineteenth century, demonstrates. Height: 15 inches

OPPOSITE:

Tobacco smoking became very popular in China during the Ch'ing dynasty, and with it came the taking of snuff. These tiny snuff bottles were carried in the sleeve, and snuff was taken with a tiny spoon made of ivory, jade, or silver. The bottles were made of such materials as wood, brass, quartz, glass, porcelain, jade, ivory, and amber. Average height: 3 inches

This superb jade carving in white nephrite, called the "calendar of beasts," was presented to the Ch'ien-lung emperor (r. 1736–1795) as a birthday gift. Surrounding the central yin-yang symbol are the twelve animals of the Chinese zodiac. On the reverse side are auspicious trigrams of the I-Ching, or Book of Changes. Width: 12 inches

In Indian and early Chinese Buddhist images, Shakyamuni Buddha is often shown seated on a "lion throne."
In this way, lions came to be regarded as protectors of the faith. Over the centuries, sculptures of lions (sometimes
called "Fu-dogs") gradually lost their savage mien and became more benign in appearance, until they began
to look like big stylized dogs; during this time they also became more secular and ornamental. This nineteenth-
century pair of lions probably stood at the entrance to a home or sacred building. Height: 20 inches

OPPOSITE:

The dancing lion is a traditional figure at the Chinese New Year celebration. A long, cloth body (not shown)
that hides several dancers is attached to the head, which is made of papier-maché and has a hinged jaw that flaps
ferociously. This dancing lion was made in Hong Kong but used in the United States. Width: 34¼ inches

In the late Ming and Ch'ing periods the horse was often associated with the monkey in a popular rebus or visual pun with the auspicious meaning "May you immediately be elevated to the rank of marquis." With the great period of Chinese trade with Southeast Asia in the thirteenth and fourteenth centuries, some cultural exchange also took place, and it is possible that the monkey in this jade piece might thus represent Hanuman, from the Ramayana. Height: 4¼ inches

OPPOSITE:

Chinese children were sometimes given toys during the great festivals. This festival tiger, made from painted fabric, reflects the tradition seen in folk arts—particularly painting—of the Ch'ing period. It was collected in 1903 by the German anthropologist Berthold Laufer. Height: 5 inches

This pair of bronze horses, of Shang or early Chou dynasty date, provides tantalizing clues to the relationship of the Siberian "animal style" to Bronze Age China. Although the casting of these horses does not exhibit the technical proficiency of the mature Shang ritual vessels, the naturalism seen in them is remarkable in the context of the usually quite stylized ritual bronze vessels. Height: 4½ inches

These two small horselike creatures of cast bronze were collected from Ordos Nomads on the northwestern Chinese frontier. They probably date back two to three thousand years. Many such bronzes were created by the non-Chinese nomads living on the northern borders. Height: both 3 inches

On the morning of the wedding day, the bride is carried in the groom's family's wedding chair to her new home. The costliness of the chair enhances the status of the groom; the bride's family follows carrying the dowry for public display. This nineteenth-century bridal palanquin with detachable panels is made with inlaid kingfisher feathers, copper wire, glass, gilt, and other materials. It is from South China. Height: 215 inches

OPPOSITE:

Detail of the wedding chair

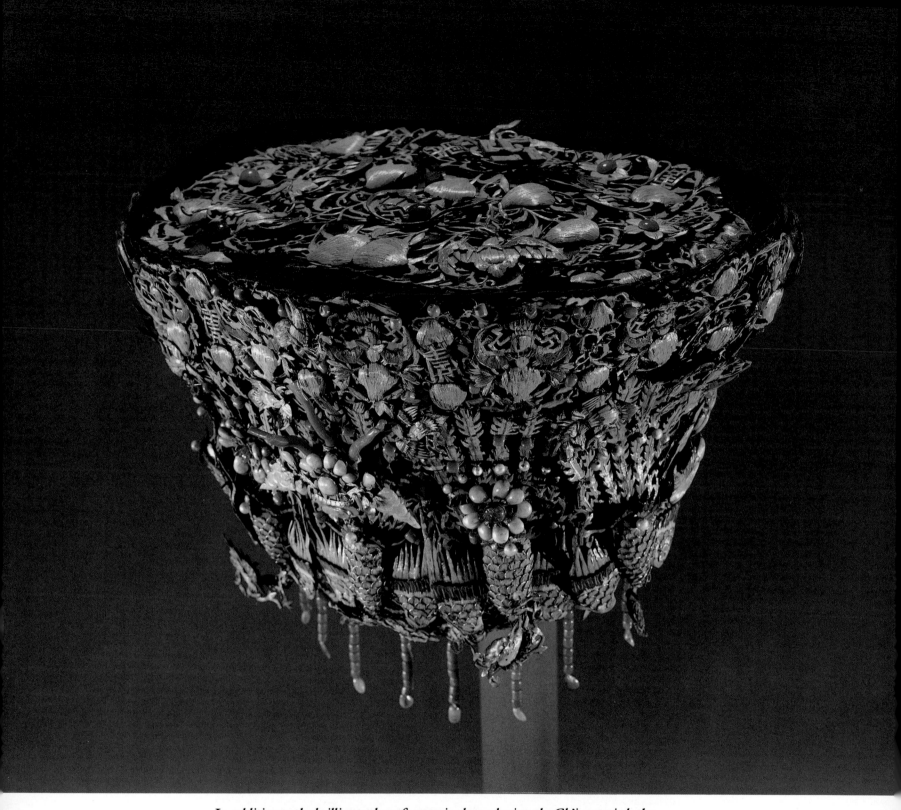

In addition to the brilliant colors of ceramic glazes during the Ch'ing period, the Chinese chose bright colors for jewelry and other personal trappings as well. This hat, probably produced by a master craftsman in South China, is decorated with kingfisher feathers, cloudy amber, jade, moonstone, and coral. Kingfisher feathers were used at least as early as the T'ang period (A.D. 618–907) for rich blues and turquoises, and tended to be used in all periods when bright colors were preferred. Height: 12 inches

This rather enigmatic photograph may be of a "secondary wife" or concubine on the bridal journey to her future home. Although she is dressed like an upper-class bride, she is riding a horse instead of a sedan chair, something that would be unthinkable and degrading for a legitimate Chinese bride. (1917)

(text continued from page 156)

side are the ancestor halls where the family records are kept and where the ancestral tablets are stored. These halls are architecturally the most splendid buildings of the community and may contain images of Taoist or Buddhist deities or saints. Here the village elders may discuss the affairs of the community. The rich colors—gold on red, gold on black lacquer, soft blues, pinks, and vivid greens—coupled with the lavish use of ideographs and traditional designs, make ancestor halls a striking relief from the rather drab building interiors and exteriors of the usual Chinese village. Combined here are ancestral records, religious images, and secular activities in a setting as splendid as the village can afford.

A striking symbol of the essential unity of Chinese society in the south is the ancestor hall. For not only is the hall a place of worship and rite, but it is a statement of familial cooperation. Ideally, any family member bearing the family name, no matter how remote the actual relationship, can find support by going to the ancestor hall. A poor family may obtain loans in terms of tools, seed, and even some money, to be repaid once

These Chinese women wear the Ch'ang-Shan, a long gown that buttons in a flap across the chest.

the crisis is past. The quarrel between families in the village can be resolved by discussion in the ancestor hall, where living elders and respected deceased provide judgment.

The ancestor hall, as a place of records, preserves not only the evidence for familial forebears but, because of reference to accomplishment in the Confucian sense, places the family firmly into the whole of China itself. In the West, in modern times at least, men are very much aware that they are members of a larger group called a nation. In general, to call oneself American, British, Spanish, Italian, Indian, or Pakistani seems to identify the individual among, say, groups of Russians, Swedes, or Australians. But within such nations there is another division based on geographical and historical premises, such as New Englander, Welshman, Basque, Venetian, Bengali, or Punjabi. For the Chinese, such divisions are not nearly so meaningful as they are in the above cases. Ultimately, no matter where one's birth or residence, a person is Chinese.

To be Chinese is not simply a matter of birth or location, but an acknowledgment that one is part of an essential stream originating in a somehow idyllic remote past, and flowing over and through vicissitudes to the present and beyond. To be Chinese is somehow to be privileged, not because the rest of the world is barbarous, though historically that idea existed among the Chinese, but because there is an inevitability about China that, in terms of human accomplishment, endures to the extent of challenging mortality itself. Only ancient Egypt seems to have possessed this temporal quality, but the pharaohs are long dead and the Chinese ethos is very much a part of the modern world.

During the Han dynasty (206 B.C.–A.D. 220), it was the custom to send princesses beyond the Great Wall to be married to leading chiefs of China's perennial enemy, the Hsiung-Nu (Huns). Indeed, throughout much of Chinese history marriage of highborn women to leaders of bordering states was the expedient taken to insure peaceful relations. Not unlike the Habsburgs of Europe, for whom the motto *Bella gerant alii, tu felix Austria nube* (Let others make wars, you, fortunate Austria, marry) was coined, Chinese emperors generally used matrimony or other peaceful means, rather than military force, to protect China's borders. This policy was, of course, rooted in the powerful Chinese sense of home, the land, the knowledge that the indigenous past validated the present for the future, and in the stated axiom that the men of Han, as they called themselves, were superior to those unfortunates who were not Chinese. For beyond China were the bar-

Women of China's Manchu ruling class dressed in traditional garb are shown here with characteristic hairstyles. The fingernail guards were a sign of nobility or high social standing. Unlike the ethnic Chinese, Manchu women did not bind their feet; platform shoes allowed the feet to be hidden by the skirt, thus giving the impression of small feet. (before 1912)

barian horse nomads, the pastoralists who lived in felt tents and shifted with the seasons like the rootless birds of the air. In such a context, there is no wonder that the tears shed by the Chinese princess, as she was borne off from China's silk-and-lacquer realm to the Huns' world of wool, leather, and sour milk, were more than the tears natural to homesickness and to the lament of the lonely in an alien world. For whoever leaves China is like a helpless baby tossed into the endless waters of the ocean.

Buddhism was well established in China by the fourth century A.D., but early encountered both Chinese ethnocentrism and the deep-seated Chinese belief in the relativity of present life to what was or is. The esoteric aspects of Buddhism as practiced in India did not take hold among the people of China, for ideas of reincarnation and Nirvana were not consistent with the linearities of the ancestor cult. What did take hold as the most popular form of Buddhism was Pure Land, which conceives of an infinite number of Buddha worlds, one of them ruled over by the Buddha Amitabha. This is a paradise world often depicted in Buddhist painting as a place of glorious palaces and splendid gardens where the blessed are in peace and happiness. According to simple practice, one could attain that blessed land by invoking Amitabha by merely uttering his name. The temples and monasteries of Chinese Buddhism were filled with the iconographies of the Pure Land and meditation upon that land was standard practice.

Even Chinese families of modest means could rent an elaborate sedan chair to transport the bride to the groom's home. In this procession, with a chair probably rented for the occasion, the bride's family and carriers precede her, carrying her dowry. When a Chinese bride stepped out of the wedding chair at the groom's house, it was often the first time they had ever seen each other. (turn of century)

Cottage industries were a common feature of rural China. In the cotton-growing areas, spinning and weaving were prime sources of supplementary income for poor families. When industrial textile machinery of western origin replaced the foot-powered spinning wheel, many spinners suffered.

This manifestation of popular attitudes toward religion marks the story of China after the Classic Age. Buddhist, Taoist, and Confucian beliefs become intermingled with local beliefs in ghosts, spirits, and mythical creations. The Goddess of Mercy, Kwan Yin, originates in the Bodhisattva Avalokitesvara, Lord of Mercy. She becomes both a moderator in the Court of Yama, King of Hell and judge of all men, and a deity of fertility. Dragon lore derives from the observance of the vitalism in nature, which is central to Taoist belief, and soon there are dragon kings, dragon boats, dragon deities, and a dragon of the sky that chases sun and moon at the Chinese New Year. There are also gate deities, star gods, peaches for longevity, bats for prosperity, tortoises for reliability, phoenixes for good fortune, war gods, and the Eight Immortals who run the gamut of wisdom, good fortune, and the performance of good for mankind.

This bewildering complexity means that the Chinese, who had to face the realities of this world, enlisted a host of supernatural helpers. Although man is indeed the link between heaven and earth, past and future, there is no question that the factors of fortune and misfortune are the chance elements in an otherwise logical world. The famous *I Ching,* or *Book of Changes,* acknowledged for thousands of years as one of the most important books confirming man's place in the cosmos, deals directly with the chance factor. For any happening is not the consequence of intellect or aware senses but the manifestation of all that is in the changing world at that moment. A bird sings here while out there, beyond sight, waves rise and fall in the vastness of ocean, while a child eats a candy over there, and a mother cries here, and a cat washes herself unseen beyond the door, and so on and on . . . . What made that moment? Are all these things in conjunction chance? How can they be measured? The *I Ching,* in effect, not only measures chance but sets forth predictabilities far more meaningful than the law of averages of the West, for

The Avenue of the Animals leads to the magnificent tombs of the Ming emperors of China. The marble statues are in pairs, one standing and one kneeling, and are symbolically meant to serve the emperors in the afterlife. (Roy Chapman Andrews, 1918)

they relate to wisdom itself. No wonder that popular Chinese religion uses the hexagrams of the *I Ching* almost as frequently as the gold-on-red characters used for good fortune and happiness.

During the latter part of the nineteenth century, many Chinese males came to the western United States to serve as workmen in such industries as lumbering, railroading, and mining. Their intention was to remain as long as was necessary to make their fortunes and then return to China. Frugal, hardworking, bound by familial links, unable to speak English, and feeling terribly isolated from China, they lived in a stressful condition. This was made even more difficult by the Americans' growing antagonism, caused not only by the Chinese "strangeness," but also by the fact that the Chinese did not intend to remain and become Americans. Competition over jobs led eventually to race riots in a number of cities and a persecution that is one of the most shameful pages in American history.

Another acute problem existed for the Chinese—the chaotic situation in their homeland. In the late nineteenth century, the Ch'ing dynasty (1644–1911), a Manchu dynasty, was struggling against civil disorder and colonialism. The population in China was rapidly increasing and, in spite of intensive cultivation of the soil, famine, accompanied by plague and other diseases, was all too frequent. Many Chinese migrated from north to south and then on into Southeast Asia and the islands of Indonesia, and some came to the New World. As conditions in China worsened, it became obvious to many Chinese in America that a return to China was impractical. They sent for their families and settled more and more into Chinese communities in cities such as San Francisco, Seattle, and

OPPOSITE:

Popular Chinese drama reached a high point in Peking in the nineteenth century. Characters in Chinese theater are classified into various categories and types. At right is lao-sheng, *the righteous, bearded old man. The color and design of the costume denote the character type: emperors are dressed in yellow, old people in brown, high officials of good character in red, and rough characters in black. The actors with shaved foreheads may have had painted-face roles* (hua-lien), *which required complicated makeup. The one woman in this photograph, a type called* tan, *may actually be a man; as in Elizabethan drama, classical Chinese theater traditionally used males for all roles. (probably turn of century)*

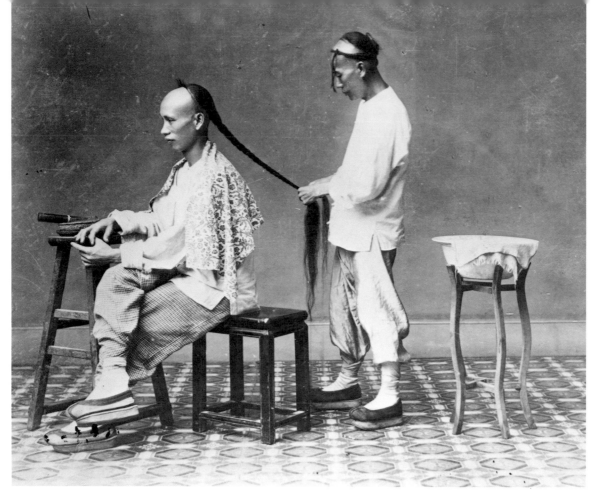

The Manchu rulers of China (1644–1912) required their subjects to wear their hair in queues as a symbol of submission to the emperor. Itinerant barbers prepared the queue by shaving parts of the head and braiding the remaining hair. The queue became a rallying point for the Chinese who rebelled against the Manchu dynasty, and the rebels who refused to wear them were called "long hairs." When the Manchu dynasty was overthrown in 1912, the new republican government ordered all queues to be cut off. (before 1912)

Peking carpenters construct a house using simple hand-held tools for sawing, shaping, and hammering.

New York. Here they built prosperous businesses, including famous restaurants. Criminal clans rooted in China had a growing membership in these Chinatowns, where they blackmailed the other Chinese, introducing vice, gambling, and opium dens just as in China. Rivalries among these clans led to wars, known to the Americans as tong wars; these were bloody, and because terrorist tactics were used against peaceful Chinese, the police could do little about them, for people were afraid of informing. Eventually the Chinese themselves brought an end to the problem.

Chinatowns were regarded as extremely dangerous areas where no one ventured without suitable protection—night or day. It augmented an already deep-seated prejudice and led to the infamous Exclusion Laws. Like the Chinese princess sent into Mongolia, many Chinese in America went through an agony of identity crisis. They could not go back to a China where for many there was no hope of living even reasonably well, and they could not remain in a country where even their children were threatened.

The China sustaining the immigrant Chinese in America is composed of many things, above all the durability of the family, the cooperation of the community, and an inherent sense that China will endure whether as nation or as heartfelt mystique. Today, many young Chinese, in the tradition of the wise of old China, have made scholarship their tactic. For others, their work is to a very real extent dependent on how far that occupation takes them from other Chinese. For with the loss of community, a fundamental element in Chinese identity is lost. It is another step away from the China that has played such a significant role in the wholeness of man's earthly experience, a step not easily taken. To believe one understands its gravity is presumptuous for anyone but a Chinese. Confucius has said it with the utmost grace: "The humane man, desiring to be established himself, seeks to establish others; desiring himself to succeed, he helps others to succeed. To judge others by what one knows of oneself is the method of achieving humanity."

JAPAN'S KAMI

THE BEST WAY TO APPROACH JAPAN is not from the east, crossing by sea from the coasts of the New World as did the ships of Commodore Perry, but from the west, from China and Korea, or out of the hot lands of the southern Indies. Then Japan and the Japanese take on a historical and esthetic clarity that makes understandable a special world, understandable, that is, in an Asian context. For Japan is the end of Asia. Beyond it lies the vast Pacific Ocean, crossable by traditional craft only on the north where the west-east current of Japan wafts fishing boats to the Aleutians and into the mists of the lands of Tlingit, Haida, and Kwakiutl Indians.

Lying on the eastern fringe of the great Eurasian landmass, Japan through its culture expresses its rich debt both to the great traditions of China and India, which historically have influenced it, and to its own indigenous culture. The most industrialized Asian nation, Japan is a tribute to the native genius of seizing on another's invention and turning it into a world commodity. Modern Japan presents a picture of slick, efficient, profitable, modern enterprise. At the end of World War II, I saw men who carried empty briefcases into empty offices and made calls on disconnected phones. Why, I asked, did they do so? The answer was always so that they would be ready when the time came for real work!

Now the briefcases are filled, the offices have multiplied enormously, and the telephones ring, ring, ring—and are interminably answered. Japan bustles with activity, and there is hardly a country in the world that does not possess Japanese products in quantity. Nearly annihilated by the fires caused by militarism, with the dream of the unconquered shattered and young men's bodies scattered from Rabaul to Manila, the China Sea, and beyond, Japan arose out of chaos and now literally commands the world's trade. Whatever the reasons for this resurrection out of hell, nothing commands the world's

The sacred Mt. Fuji is famous for its beauty; its snowcapped symmetrical shape, surrounded by lakes and forests, has inspired Japanese artists and poets for centuries. The man in the boat is wearing the traditional Japanese farmer's raincoat, a cloak of matted straw. (probably late 19th or early 20th century)

respect more than economic success, for everything is supposed to follow—happy home-life, esthetic triumph, tranquility, and peace of mind. But as has been the case in so many nations of the world, all these were not the consequence of industrial triumph. For Japan has had the same problems as other modern nations: growing drug abuse, alcoholism, and crime; youth disaffection; environmental pollution; and corruption in industry and government. Increasingly there seems little for the individual to rely on that is tradition-ally Japanese. The emperor denies his divinity, the class structure is eroding, most Jap-anese live in nuclear families in cities, mass media assault traditional values, and simplistic third-class popular reading mocks the potential of the language.

Japan's best writers reflect the problem and in doing so describe what is true of modern Asia itself. It can be summarized as a search for identity and with it a sense that that identity may never be found. The themes of much of Japanese writing of the last hundred years are concerned with change. One writer, despairing over the loss of old Japanese values, finds them remaining only in geisha girls. Despising them intrinsically, yet he shows them as tragic figures cast out of time and in so doing portrays the dilemma of finding the Japanese self in the modern world. Another writer tells a heartbreaking story of young men moving off to the city, to a foreign country, and leaving young women to face lives with no hope of emancipation. Still another reiterates the mindless, daily life of the industrial laborer. Obsession is a constant theme where the individual finds identity only in the monotonous pursuit of an object or a person until the achievement is made . . . and then there is nothing else. One of the most celebrated of Yukio Mishima's novels recounts the story of a young priest who, obsessed with the beauty of the famous Golden Pavilion of Yoshimitsu, in the end burns it to the ground. Some Japanese see in this an allegory in that the love for Japan, held in the past with such fervor, required finally the destruction brought by World War II. Then the Japanese soulless wanders in a technological nightmare. A number of Japan's leading writers have committed suicide. Mishima himself performed the act as if he were a samurai warrior demonstrating by his death the loss of the old values of honor and service, a loss characteristic of modern Japan. And he made it known that his appeal was to the emperor.

There was a famous trial not long ago that hinged on the question of old versus new values in Japan. For a number of years a chemical plant had dumped poisonous waste into the sea, affecting the fish that were basic to the diet of a number of fishing villages in the vicinity. Consequently many villagers became sick, some fatally so. It took a long while before the case reached the government courts where the villagers at last were able to confront the industrialists. After industry's usual defense about the need for more exact proof of the deadly food chain and its relationship to the chemical plant, and the follow-up that the plant provided many jobs and was necessary to the national economy, one old villager asked the representatives of management: "Are you Japanese?" For the poisoned fish, the reiterated pain of chemical illness, and the failure of industry to listen were not important. What counted for the villager was the essential spirit, a way of doing, of thinking, of interrelating that was Japanese. This pattern of spirit, of man, and

The grand torii *of the island shrine of Miyajima is considered to be one of the most beautiful views in Japan. The shrine, which is located on the inland sea near Hiroshima, was founded in ancient times and restored in the Fujiwara period (868–1185). (Bruce Hunter, recent)*

Archery was not only a form of weaponry in Japan, but also a way to discipline the mind and body during Zen Buddhist training. Japanese bows are very large— some medieval ones measure nine feet in length. This photograph of the Japanese archer S. Kuwayama was taken in the American Museum of Natural History as part of a series illustrating Japanese archery. (H.J. Price, 1932)

of land was time-honored. To be Japanese was to respect this life pattern and all else would follow.

What was and is this spirit? As so often, there is no direct answer, but there is a partial one, an inkling, as it were. It starts with an obvious fact—Japan is a beautiful country. Four mountain-crowned islands surrounded by ocean and sea extend over twenty degrees latitude. Its crescent shape links it with Korea and eastern Siberia, yet it touches neither. Japan is subject to earthquakes and tidal waves. It is not a quiet, sea-girt paradise with tropical seas, but a land of great contrasts: high mountains and stony beaches; volcanoes and sandy littorals; rock promontories in the sea and mossy stones in clear streams; pristine green forests and untold miles of rice paddies. By day, Japan's nature feeds the eye and provokes the mind; by night, there are elements of darkness and light that motivate the sensitive to remember the past.

Consciousness of the past is an element of the Japanese spirit. Unlike the West, where conceptions of earlier times are dominated by great figures such as Pericles, Alexander, Elizabeth I, and Napoleon, the Japanese tend to think of the past as a sequence of events and of dynastic or dominating families. To be sure, there are great men— warriors, rulers, priests, artists, thinkers—but they tend to be regarded as products of their time rather than creators of it. In this sense, history for the Japanese has a kind of logic that emphasizes durability through time rather than uncertainty and the vagaries of direction caused by individual personalities. Not unlike the earthquake-prone country-side, Japanese history sways with the movements of events but remains paradoxically stable. There were no foreign rulers, no Mongol or Manchu dynasties. But there has been a continual struggle between local rule and centralized government, between parties of secular and sacred authority, and between conservative champions of tradition and progressive proponents of other ways of doing and thinking. Yet one senses in Japanese history its evolutionary rather than revolutionary qualities.

Japan's extended prehistory consists of a culture based on hunting, gathering, and fishing, with people living in semisubterranean houses near shores of a stream, lake, or sea, and making a cord-impressed pottery that is very elaborate in shape and pattern. Rather strange but exuberant clay figurines (*dogū*) were also in the cord-impressed style. One gains the impression of formalities in social organization based on function and wealth that are found in tribal systems in other parts of the world. Japanese agricultural activity begins after 300 B.C. with rice cultivation. In use were bronze and iron tools, and the knowledge of their manufacture came largely from the Han dynasty in China. Household village clusters near cultivable fields were the settlement patterns, as they were to be for hundreds of years.

There seems to have been little centralization in this prehistoric period, but after A.D. 300, with the advent of Central and East Asian influence of considerable scale, the farming settlements fell increasingly under the influence of an aristocracy. Society was more and more divided into two great groups: the aristocracy and their clans with their special deities; and the people in turn divided by function, such as farmers, fishermen, and specialized craftsmen. These occupational groups were attached to the aristocratic clans, giving the impression of an incipient feudalism.

One of these clans, the Yamato, was dominant, and its patron was the Sun Goddess Amaterasu. Her grandson, Ninigi no Mikoto, is said to have descended to earth to found the imperial house, which began with Jimmu in 660 B.C. according to the mythological calendar. Most likely the clan leaders of Yamato gained greater and greater authority, and with increased contact with China eventually emulated China's imperial concept so that it is possible that the first true emperors of Japan did not arrive on the scene until about A.D. 500 By true emperor in the Eastern sense one means an individual who has divine origins and/or status. In Japan, this divinity came via the Sun Goddess myth. To this day, the shrine at Ise, dedicated to the Sun Goddess, is maintained by complete renewal every twenty years. It is the seat of the mirror, one of the three treasures sent to earth with Ninigi no Mikoto by the Sun Goddess as token of the founding of the imperial house. The present emperor Hirohito is the 124th in direct line from Jimmu.

Buddhism came to Japan from Korea about A.D. 552 and with it an augmenting contact with China that brought much of Chinese thought and accomplishment. In particular, Chinese characters became the basis for the written language. Some fifty characters, the antecedents of *kana*, acted as syllabary symbols for the native Japanese, but the Chinese written vocabulary was so large and appropriate for expression that the Japanese kept *both* Chinese ideographs and the early *kana*. (True *kana* emerged in the tenth century.)

The court of Japan was very sophisticated in the eighth century, a time when Asia, both east and west, achieved cultural levels of the highest quality. The Japanese capital was Nara, a city that, miracle of miracles, still exists, and where one can enter ancient temples almost as if the world outside were an illusion. But Nara's prominence as a capital city lasted less than one hundred years. In 794, while Charlemagne was ruling Europe, the capital was moved to Heian, or Kyoto, which was more central for the rule of the provinces. It is there that the center of power was situated for nearly eight hundred years.

In Kyoto, the Fujiwara family essentially took over the rulership of Japan, first as regents to the emperors, and then as virtual dictators who relegated the emperors to tokenism. Under the Fujiwara the country flourished. Most notable were the brilliant writings of court ladies, among which Lady Murasaki's *Tale of Genji* is outstanding. This superb account of court life in Heian times evokes qualities of humanity that go far beyond time and place. Students of Japanese culture refer to a quality inherent in the novel called *aware*. As with so many of the terms derived from Asian literature, the English equivalent is never exact. The term has changed through time, but it refers essentially to the sensitivity a cultivated individual has to the harmonies within nature, within human relationships. These are wonderfully described in Lady Murasaki's story: we see the fan before a lady's face and the shadows on the still water as a courtier goes by; we smell the delicate odors of a Heian garden and hear the titter of laughter. The court

Japanese farms were traditionally very small; at the turn of the century well over 90 percent of all farms were less than five acres, with every square foot cultivated. Since beasts of burden require land and fodder, most labor is done by the members of the family. Here a farmer operates an irrigation wheel for a rice paddy. (c. 1920)

Japan is a mountainous country and very little of its land is cultivable. The growing of rice, the staple crop, is restricted to the alluvial floors, deltas, and intermontane basins that cover less than 20 percent of the rugged, tectonic island chain. Japanese women usually plant rice. (c. 1920)

nobles muse over the qualities of feminine beauty with Genji, "The Shining Prince," who is the essence of all that is perfect in a man, at their head. Love is a paramount theme and courtly love is the manner by which the highest romance can be obtained. In the end, when we have lived through the experiences of the characters, we come away with an exquisite sense of sadness that all changes, that there is no perfection possible from man's resources. *Aware*, then, refers to a sensitivity to the mortality of things that are flower-like in their delicacy, yet profoundly meaningful in the sum of human experience.

The Fujiwara court was highly refined, strictly structured, and in the end incapable of dealing with the realities imposed by economic demands, frontier problems, internal familial disputes, and the struggle for power of ambitious leaders.

It is during the eleventh century that the names Taira and Minamoto come into prominence. These were provincial rulers with some lineage connections to the imperial family, who had control of the marshlands—the Taira in the west and center, the Minamoto in what later would be the Tokyo region. The Taira and Minamoto clans grew to hate one another, and their contending begins some four hundred years of Japanese feudalism. The Taira first dominated and attempted to rule, as did the Fujiwara, from Kyoto, but at the naval battle of Dan-no-ura the Minamoto broke Taira power and established a military control known as the shogunate. Ostensibly receiving their authority from the emperor, the shoguns in actuality operated fairly much on their own volition. The nobility of Genji's type in the Fujiwara heyday remained in Kyoto, increasingly remote from the realities of rulership but still cultivating the poetry and graphic arts that gave them their particular identity. Gradually, they too merged with the warrior society which was the dominant force of medieval Japan.

This society, summarized by the term samurai (one who serves), was characterized by military ability, intense loyalty to leaders, and a personal pride reaching the level of arrogance. As provincial warriors they contrasted sharply with the courtiers of Kyoto. The wars, intrigues, and successions involving the samurai were the basis of some of the most popular stories known to the Japanese. Like the cowboy stories of the American West, many modern Japanese concepts of history are samurai centered.

In particular, the tale of Yoshitsune, a prince of the Minamoto, and his giant friend and ally, Benkei, is one of great popularity. The young boy has been placed deliberately in a monastery, safe from the clutches of the Taira rulers who have vowed to finish off the Minamoto. There are many versions of the story. One tells how the Tengu King, the birdlike, long-nosed goblin, taught Yoshitsune swordsmanship. Already accomplished in flute playing, the young prince was an adept pupil. His final examination was to fight the Tengu King himself, and when he proved better than his master he knew he was ready to leave his exile. In his wanderings he encounters Benkei, a giant priest, who has restlessly wandered the countryside encountering all kinds of adventures in which he inevitably comes out on top owing to his enormous strength. But this time he is no match for the skilled swordsmanship of Yoshitsune, even though he himself has learned the martial art from a master. Consequently Benkei, in good samurai fashion, pledges himself to Yoshitsune. Then follows the story of the growth in power of the reviving Minamoto who, under Yoshitsune's brother Yoritomo, challenge and defeat the Taira. It is said that Yoshitsune actually led the Minamoto forces at Dan-no-ura. But Yoritomo, increasingly jealous of his younger brother's fame, drives Yoshitsune from his court and has him ruthlessly pursued along with Benkei and Yoshitsune's wife, Shizuka. In all, the story illustrates the samurai qualities of prowess, courage, and loyalty.

Despite such qualities during the long period of military domination, many shogun and their provincial governors (*daimyo*) were patrons of the arts. Painting, such as that of the world-famous Sesshu, and architecture, such as that of the Gold and the Silver Pavilions, are outstanding. The Nō theater, the tea ceremony, and even landscape gardening gained great prominence. Whereas in the previous Fujiwara court there had been an increasingly rigid esthetic etiquette, the feudal age was looser and permitted innovation.

Relations between the shogun and his *daimyo* were always tense, for self-interest was the rule. Paradoxically, this may have contributed significantly to the growth of new techniques in crafts and the development of new esthetic motivations. Gradually many *daimyo* gained greater autonomy as the shogunate powers weakened, particularly the Ashikaga shoguns, successors to the heirs of the Minamoto. Castle-towns, like those of Europe in medieval times, dotted the landscape in the midst of agriculturally fruitful tracts and on

(text continued on page 197)

This splendid wooden figure of Jizō, the Japanese Buddhist patron-protector of warriors, travelers, and especially children, stands on a lotus pedestal. One of the best-loved of all Japanese deities, he holds the sacred jewel (tama) in his left hand, and staff with rings (shakujō) in his right hand. He is usually portrayed as a young monk with a shaved head and holding the attributes seen here. Height: 35 inches

The term mandala *usually refers to a schematic representation of the Two Worlds, spiritual and material, as viewed by the Shingon sect of Buddhism. The term is also applied to paintings of the type shown here, of the Pure Land Jōdō sect. These paintings show a central architectural complex set within a landscape scene. Although the painting is Japanese, the figures of the various deities wear Indian costume. The painting, a portion of which is shown here, is dated 1491. Dimensions: 49 x 32 inches*

OPPOSITE:

This seated wooden deity with six arms is known in the Shingon sect of Buddhism as Aizen Myō-ō, often thought of as the god of love. He is more accurately described as the destroyer of vulgar passions while striving to replace them with a form of universal love that offers salvation. Shingon, or the "True Word" sect of Buddhism, held art in high esteem and felt that paintings and sculpture, as seen here, were necessary vehicles for the transmission of the way toward enlightenment. Height: 31 inches

186

This nineteenth-century comical mask is based on the original Usobuki *mask found in* Kyōgen, *the comic-farcical interlude that always appears between two serious Nō plays. Height: 8 inches*

OPPOSITE:

Haniwa *are terra-cotta images representing architectural, animal, and human forms. They are usually found at the burial mounds of Japanese rulers during the period between c. 300 to 600 A.D. They may have been meant either to guard the tomb or accompany the dead. Height: 8 inches*

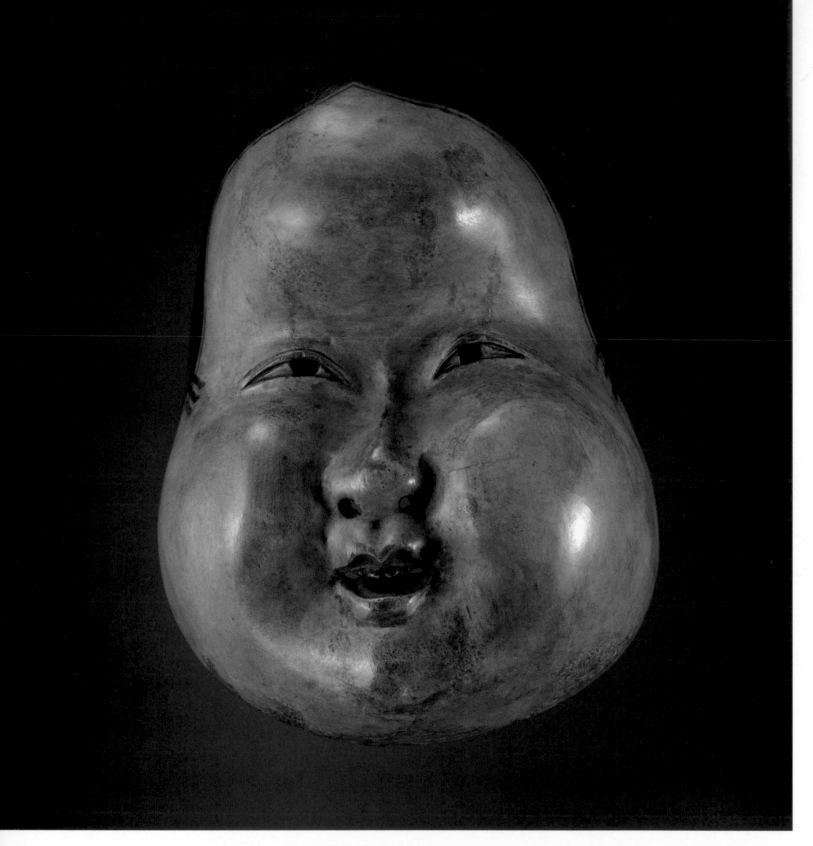

The nature of the Kyōgen masks was based on the exaggeration of particular features to accentuate the farce. This fat-cheeked personage is called Oto *or* Otafuku. *Height: 8 inches*

OPPOSITE:

Netsukes are small, sculpted images that developed in the Edo period (1615–1867). They come in many shapes and sizes, and illustrate scenes from the traditional literature of Japan. They were worn as a toggle attached by a cord looped through the sash of the kimono, attached to small boxes or pouches. Their use died out when western clothing became popular after 1868, and many netsuke carvers turned to creating export wares. This ivory example is of Shōki, the demon queller, who is trying to keep three demons in a barrel. It is signed by Gyokkō, a sculptor who worked between 1830 and 1867. Height: 2½ inches

OPPOSITE:

This nineteenth-century ivory okimono *shows an entertainer and his young assistant about to start a street performance. Height: 6 inches*

In Japanese, okimono *usually refers to any "large" carved object, which in Japan is usually rather small. This ivory* okimono *depicting a farmer spearing a bird probably stood in the* tokonoma, *or alcove, of the main room. When Japan began trading extensively with the west in the nineteenth century,* okimono *became particularly valuable export objects. Most were made during the Meiji period (1868–1912). Height: 3 inches*

OPPOSITE:

Here, a nineteenth-century ivory netsuke shows two tiny figures struggling to carry an oversized "Daruma Doll," symbolic of good luck. Daruma, a legendary monk, brought to China from India a form of Buddhism the Japanese call Zen. According to legend, he meditated so long that he lost the use of his arms and legs. The carving is signed by Hūichi. Height: 2 inches

Ashinaga *(Long Legs)* and Tenaga *(Long Arms),* originally Chinese folklore characters, *also appear in Japanese legends. They form a perfect symbiotic relationship. Long Arms sits atop Long Legs' shoulders, and they both venture into deep water to catch the fish necessary for their diet. This netsuke is of carved wood. Height: 7 inches*

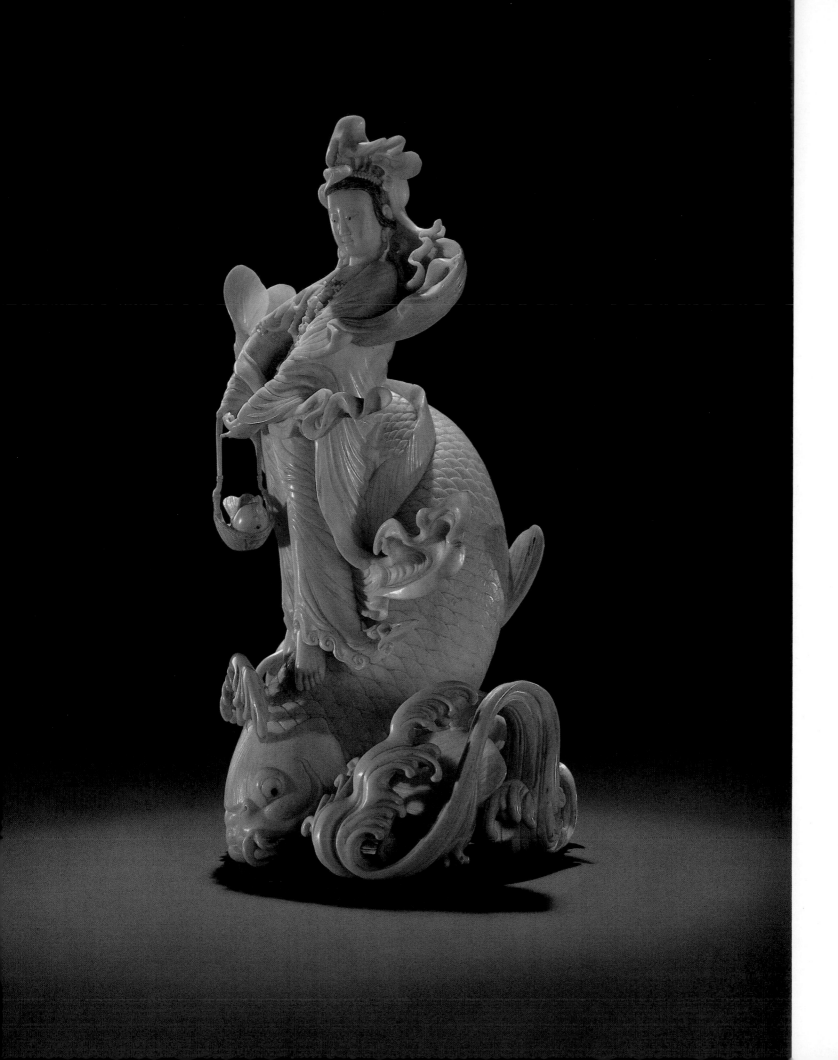

(text continued from page 184)

routes with economic advantages. Of interest was the growing role of Portuguese traders and European commerce generally and with it the advent of Christianity.

The tension between local self-rule and central authority had a paradoxical quality in that all acknowledged the divine roots of the imperial line and the essential spirit (or kami) of Japan. The natural tendency of the Japanese was toward unification, not separatism, and was instrumental in the success of powerful leaders (Nobunaga, Hideyoshi, and Tokugawa Ieyasu) in eventually reunifying Japan. Of these, Tokugawa Ieyasu was the founder of the Tokugawa shogunate which was to rule Japan until 1867 and was the beginning of intensive Westernization under the Emperor Meiji. Ieyasu controlled the *daimyo* by moving them about: residence on an alternative basis in the shogunate capital Edo (Tokyo) was required of all *daimyo*. The dangers of merchants causing unrest were offset by reinforcing the active class system which placed the warriors at the top, followed by the two producing occupations, farmers and artisans, leaving the merchant at the bottom. The Tokugawa family personally held a quarter of all the agricultural land as well as having control of key cities. Thus the economic viability of their administration was insured. The peasants were held to the land, which gave stability to agricultural production, and to the protecting lord, who was responsible for his peasant subjects. He was required to protect them from banditry and from the excesses of arbitrary taxes or tribute.

Fearing a growing European presence that might support recalcitrant *daimyo*, particularly in the west remote from Edo, and fearing the challenge of Christianity to Japanese values, the Tokugawa excluded all but a few Europeans and Chinese, who in turn remained in Nagasaki. This exclusion policy effectively isolated Japan from the West for over two hundred years. But these were years of considerable development: cities and towns grew, agriculture expanded, and money became the means of exchange.

The cultural innovations of the feudal period flourished as never before. Puppet theater, Kabuki, and the marvelously understated haiku poems illustrated with superb woodblocks appeared. Costumes marking rank and occupation, and a preoccupation with ornamentation and fanciful calligraphy, made even the simplest shop in the market a festival of form and color amidst a tasteful riot of decorated street signs, lanterns, parasols, and door posts. This was the Japan of the floating world, of pleasure quarters, of the geisha, of Saikaku's *Five Women Who Loved Love* and Chikamatsu's love suicides. It was a world where Confucian ideals were introduced into government to insure purpose and longevity. In its best sense the Tokugawa shogunate insured peace and tranquility while providing a recognized and not totally uncreative place for everyone. The writings of the time explored Confucianism, revived interest in ancient Japan, and sought rational means of understanding the nature of government and the meaning of history.

Kannon, the Buddhist goddess of mercy, is depicted in this fine ivory okimono *that probably dates from the late nineteenth century. There are many stories about her; this carving depicts one story in which Kannon repeatedly ensnared herself in a prince's fishing net, thereby preventing the capture of fish for whom she felt compassion. Height: 6½ inches*

For those in the West who find the exclusiveness of Tokugawa Japan anathema, the fact of the matter is that Tokugawa rule grew out of the chaos of a feudal age and provided for an individual security hitherto unknown. The Tokugawa age reinforced Japanese self-identity and paradoxically prepared the way for the Westernization and modernization that were to come. For it allowed the individual to act in concert with other individuals toward a goal already manifest in well-used symbols.

The fall of the Tokugawa was presaged by two oddly contradictory factors. Under the Tokugawa the samurai had nobody to fight. Whereas they had high social status and rights possessed by no other social class, they tended to be impecunious followers of lords whose success depended not on arms but on farmers and merchants. It is commonly stated that samurai poverty motivated the arts of Zen Buddhism, the tea cult, the miniature austerities of flower arrangement, and landscape gardening. For these arts are not expensive. Rocks, sand, flowers, crudely made tea cups, lonely meditation, and the linking of poetic lines are available to even the poorest person. Refined taste, sensitivity, and the search for a richness beyond the material are all that is needed.

The other factor was the success of the merchant group, the lowest within the class structure. The growing cities and towns, the tight controls of Tokugawa administration securing the economic system, and the fundamental social and political order of the day were ideal for the role of the merchant. The exchange of goods and services by merchants was necessary if the townspeople were to have the luxury foodstuffs, cloth, metal, ceramic, paper, and wood necessary to city life. The raw materials of the craftsmen, the finished products of the artisan, and the markets necessary for their distribution could not be the responsibility of samurai. They were untrained in such matters, and such activities were

Three Japanese women of Hokkaido smoke pipes. The northern islands of Japan are forested in pine and fir, and have a climate similar to Maine's. Previously the domain of the Ainu, the islands were not heavily settled by the Japanese until the end of the shogunate in 1869. These women may be part Ainu, but they lack the characteristic lip tattoo and Caucasian features. (probably Berthold Laufer, c. 1900)

This peasant of northern Japan is dressed for hunting. (probably Berthold Laufer, c. 1900)

socially demeaning and illegal. The merchant class grew in wealth while remaining low in social standing; the samurai grew poorer while remaining high in social status. Samurai often found themselves in debt to the merchants and this caused acute discomfort.

It is no wonder that merchants increasingly looked to the outside world for the stuff of their trade while samurai intelligentsia sought for answers to their dilemma. The Tokugawa shogunate, unable to handle the growing needs of its people, sought reactionary answers, including excessive taxation on the peasantry and military ways to control *daimyo* recalcitrance. Discontent grew until, with the coming of Commodore Perry in 1854 and the breakdown of the exclusion policy, the Tokugawa system fell apart with an uprising and a civil war ending in 1869. It was replaced by the centralization of a new imperial system and the restoration of the emperor to central authority. Brought out of the secluded court at Kyoto, where practices rooted in the Fujiwara court were still maintained, Emperor Meiji made Edo the imperial seat (now called Tokyo). He thus assumed symbolically a secular shogunate role. It is significant that proud samurai supporters were troubled by this move, for it had been a long time since an emperor had been in authority and they felt that the emperor ought to remain in Kyoto handling sacred affairs, while a new shogun should be found for Tokyo to run Japan in the emperor's name.

The two recalcitrants of Tokugawa times, the samurai and the merchant, brought

Japanese society is characterized by, among other things, extreme politeness and attention to form. Traditionally divided into classes, Japanese society had well-defined modes of greeting and conduct within and between classes. The formal greeting of these women coming to call is typical of the formality that existed even between close friends of the same social class. (probably early 20th century)

By the late nineteenth century the drinking of tea had often become an opportunity for a moment of quiet relaxation, as shown in the photograph, rather than the elaborate ritual it had been in previous ages.

Ikebana, or flower arranging, is an elaborate art form in Japan that dates back to the seventh century. Although it was introduced from China as a flower offering to Buddha, it is today a formal, popular tradition that is more aesthetic than religious in meaning. Until 1868, ikebana was principally a man's occupation, reserved mostly for Buddhist priests, samurai, and noblemen. In the last century it has become very popular among Japanese women. (early 20th century)

Japan into the modern world, and, in the name of the emperor, made Japan a world power. In the end, their ambitions nearly destroyed the country as the events of World War II demonstrated. Now the social order is changing. The samurai are nearly gone, and the merchant, the lowest in the Tokugawa social scale, reigns.

Japanese history, it should be repeated, demonstrates a clearcut conflict between sacred and secular authority, a concern for a stable social order, and a strong sense of collective interest over gains to the individual. It is wonderfully clear that the arts, particularly poetry, were cultivated by many important figures in Japanese history. It is as if each sought some relationship between self, society, and nature that would explain why action was necessary and why events had to take their course.

Japanese religion is another element in this elusive spirit quality that constitutes Japanese identity. Oddly, it is not the many sects of Buddhism, ranging from Pure Land hopes of paradise to Zen emancipation from illusion, that some consider central to Japanese thought. Buddhism in the modern world has a ritual purpose, particularly for births and funerals, which keeps it flourishing. There is also modern Buddhist faith healing, which proselytizes as well as any Christian fundamentalist sect. With all the beauty of Buddhist art that graces the temples of old Japan, and even with the clean lines of Zen ritual, Japanese Buddhism has a cosmological element relating to other worlds than Japan. Buddhism cannot escape its Indian origins, and it is one reason why Buddhism in

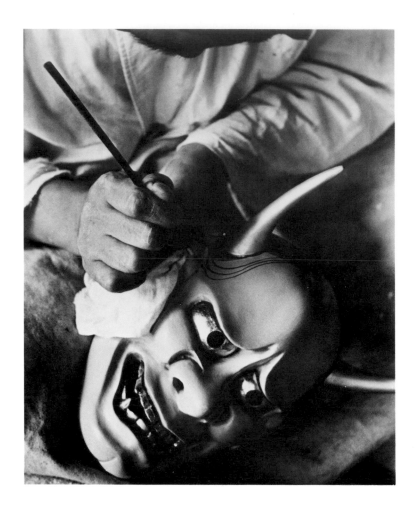

A Japanese artisan paints a mask of Hannya, representing the spirit of a jealous woman. Nō masks were originally carved by sculptors under the direct patronage of the government. The eyes of this mask, like the eyes of all Japanese supernatural-being masks, are inlaid with brass to reflect the flickering candlelight that illuminates the stage. The Nō theater, a form of masked dance-drama, originated in Japan sometime between the twelfth and fourteenth centuries. Unlike Western theater, it does not involve development through conflict; instead, all movements on stage are highly stylized. The Nō plays usually have one "first actor" who wears a mask indicating his character, and an unmasked "second actor." Both are usually assisted by companions called tsure. Nō theater draws its themes from ritual and folk dances, Buddhist scriptures, folklore, and legend. (Scopus, recent)

Japan has tried to play a political role from time to time as if to insure its Japanese roots. The role of Buddhism and its leaders is probably overstated by historians. For significant as Buddhism may have been in the formation of law and the influence on popular world view, it never seems to have held political influence for long. Its influence seems more imposed than indigenously developed.

In many Japanese homes there is a shelf referred to as a *kamidana*, or spirit shelf. On it is a simple wooden shrine containing nothing or a plain mirror, dishes for a food offering, a paper cutout called *gohei*, perhaps some paper charms, a bell, a sprig of green wood, flowers on occasion—all so simple as to be austere. This austerity, this cleanness marks Shinto with indubitable sharpness. For all its initial mystery, Shinto is not difficult to explain. But explanation is not understanding, and one has to make that distinction particularly with Shinto, for our Western intellectual arrogance assumes that explanation based on our concept of rationality makes true understanding possible. Nothing could be farther from the mark.

The term Shinto means the "Way of the Spirit, or Kami." Kami can be conceived of as a benign and elevated spirit in a world of spirits. It is at once personality within things and a quality counter to the destructive, or bad luck, elements in life. Although the Japanese are conscious of a dualism in nature, it is never as sharp as the Yin-Yang in

Chinese Taoism. The Japanese creation myth emphasizes not so much how the world was created as that it was created to make Japan possible. Even though the creator gods are male and female, Japan was made from sea drops off the god's spear, and from the descent of heirs of the Sun Goddess who founded the imperial rulership. In this linearity there is a straightforward cause and effect that does not need dualities to define it. The kami of origins is *a* good, not *two* goods. In this sense dualistic explanations for origins are not an essential theme in Shinto.

Shinto offers a means of interrelating with the elevated qualities of life. For an artist, it can be simply the glimpse of a pattern in nature; for the peasant, the well-being brought by rewarded work. Kami can be specific, as the particular shape of a teapot; it can be general, as the good fortune of being a Japanese. The *kamidana* is a means of acknowledging formally the role of the good spirit element in life.

Shinto's relationship to the emperor made possible the state Shinto prevalent in Japan from the Meiji period up to the end of World War II. When the Mongols attacked Japan in the thirteenth century, typhoons blew up and drove them away. To the Japanese, these great rescuing winds had been sent by the gods. Gods are manifest in Shinto as animistic personalities encompassing the divinity of Japan's kami origins. The winds were called *kamikaze*, a term applied to the pilots in World War II who flew suicide missions secure in the knowledge of their role's divinity. For Japan had never been conquered and it seemingly had a mission related to its divine origins. After World War II, state Shinto was abolished, but Shinto today is unquestionably still the national faith of Japan. It is a religion to live by, for its purpose is clearly to promote the best in nature. When the fisherman asked the industrialist "Are you Japanese?" he was referring to the kami that made being Japanese a particular privilege.

It is an elusive matter, this kami: a Japanese mother can take her child to a public Shinto shrine, show the baby to the kami, and while doing so pronounce the baby's name for the first time; a student might light a stick of incense at the *kamidana* before taking a test; older people might weep to see the secularized emperor. Mount Fuji has a kami, so do haiku, laughter, love, and the old tree. Almost by definition, the kami of Shinto is what gives good things their goodness, and what defines the fine qualities of life. Nothing is so necessary to Japanese identity as Shinto, whether institutional or private.

Another element in Japanese identity is knowing one's place. The anthropologist Ruth Benedict, writing of the Japanese during World War II, described a system called "On," which in essence refers to the variety of obligations assumed by a Japanese. Some are unrepayable, like the luck of being Japanese in the first place, or the obligation one has to one's parents in being born. Others are repayable, like receiving help from a friend or, in more dramatic cases, seeking revenge or saving face by committing suicide. The Benedict study is no longer completely valid, for Japan has changed. But a class consciousness rooted in the old system still prevails. In Tokugawa times, class divisions were rigidly imposed. One could not marry out of one's class. Whole patterns of behavior were observed—the depth of bow, the way one looked or did not look, and the language, where honorific forms were so prevalent that one had a wholly different way of speaking according to the class member. This had the effect of creating a social and economic symbiosis where everyone had a place, a manner, and a daily role with specific goals to fulfill. In the larger social and economic system, such interdependencies, like the caste system of India, made for a network of coherent relationships. The Tokugawa social system was a caste system, but its emphasis was on role playing and the maintenance of a characteristic Japanese sense of order rather than on ideas of purity and impurity. However, there were *eta* people outside the social system who, like the untouchables, could do menial tasks and were for all intents and purposes treated as slaves.

Essentially, the Japanese family has been a Confucian family with emphasis on patriarchy and patrilinearity. By having one son succeed to the position of household head, the Japanese household can be maintained across the generations. Younger brothers either leave the family or remain as subordinates to their older siblings. With population growth during the Tokugawa period, drift to the cities and towns took place. This required shifts in class status. Brothers or sons of farmers could not be farmers in cities. Thus numerous people attached themselves to merchants and to whatever industries or service units were available. The Tokugawa attempted to force the peasantry to stay on the land but were only partially successful in the face of population pressures. Although filial piety was respected, the Japanese rarely developed the ancestral depth and ritual prescribed for the Chinese. Clanship among the peasantry was nothing like that of the Chinese. Instead, the idea of branch families linked by ancestral ties over a few generations was prevalent.

Women in Japan have had little or no authority, even within the family. Subservience to the oldest male's authority has been the rule. Formality exists between husband and

A rural Japanese girl pauses on a road near Oshima, wearing a simple kimono and a headcovering. The kimono is secured by a sash, or obi, which is wound about the waist several times and knotted at the back. A small cushion is placed under the knot to prevent discomfort. (Roy Chapman Andrews, 1910)

OPPOSITE:

The pagoda-shaped building seen here is a structure commonly placed in a prescribed position within the Japanese Buddhist temple compound. Sacred relics were buried under the center pole, and Buddhist images were placed facing the four cardinal directions. Pilgrims walk around the building in a specified direction as they offer prayers. (Roy Chapman Andrews, 1909)

wife, and social activity is largely male to male. This has often made the geisha the only woman to whom men could speak openly and even then there are rules governing behavior. For the geisha is not intrinsically a prostitute, but a cultivated individual capable of entertaining with wit, song, dance, and manner, and providing the lacking female companionship. There are many Japanese stories of husbands neglecting their wives as the men sought fellowship away from the formalities necessary in the home.

Children, of course, made the family more cohesive. Depending on the parents' occupation, children were raised essentially to fulfill the role already laid out for them: the strict spartan upbringing necessary for samurai; the daily tasks of the farmer; the apprenticeship of the artisan. Grandparents, with their ties to past ways of doing things, gave children a sense of tradition which reinforced the work ethic and above all established the manners and customs of social relationships. Probably no Asian nation, or indeed any nation of the world, had as formal a prescribed manner of social behavior as the Japanese. One of the most famous stories of Tokugawa Japan tells of how a certain lord was misinformed by a high government official as to correct behavior at court. The lord made a slight error and was so shamed that he committed suicide. His followers in the end avenged him and then committed suicide themselves.

With Westernization, the class divisions and with them the strict behavioral patterns broke down. Up to World War II, however, both the Confucian family ethic and formality of behavior still had a significant place. Today, with more women in the work force, with most Japanese in cities, with nuclear family life in apartment houses, and with the overall effect of American-style mass media, the whole social system has undergone great change. In management-employee relationships there has been a pattern of behavior where management acts as understanding father and the employees as obedient children, but that is being replaced by standards of materialism and authority familiar in the West. The language, too, has lost much of its honorific dialect and is more standardized into common speech. Familial relationships beyond the nuclear family are still held, but grandparents are no longer authority enforcers. They are held in respect and affection, and much of the old politeness of manner remains, but much is individual choice rather than custom, even though that seeming choice retains the older forms of etiquette. Even with change, the Japanese sense of social position remains and respect is still displayed to the elderly, to the people in authority. It is clear that the Japanese ultimately respect one another. The land, the history, the faith, the work ethic, and the sense of place create an identity that each Japanese must in the end find for himself or herself. Japanese poets and writers of recent times have in their own way attempted to describe this identity. Self-respect and social respect seem to lie for the Japanese in the capability of acknowledging those elements of traditional life that have endured.

THE ASIAN
OVERVIEW

VII

OF THE MANY POSSIBLE OVERVIEWS of traditional Asian cultures, all of them have to consider the Semitic Near East, the Indo-Pakistan subcontinent, the basic ethnic homogeneity of China, and the island culture of Japan as stabilities with long indigenous cultural traditions capable of integrating alien influences without losing their original cultural character. The first three have powerful cultural influences on much of the rest of Asia, so much so as to act as founts of new accomplishment rooted in indigenous ways.

The rest of Asia can be divided into significantly different cultural zones. The first is the Siberian region from the Bering Sea to the Urals and beyond to Lapland. This is a vast area of tundra along the shores of the Arctic Ocean, and almost impenetrable coniferous forest lands to the south. The rivers flow generally north and provide thoroughfare and food for the aboriginal cultures native to the region. It is no easy land to live in for its long, severe winters, and the isolation of its parts, inhospitable to those who do not know it well. Yet there is a degree of exuberance in the successful adaptations made by Paleo-Asians to the harshness of Siberia. Some, like the Eskimo, sustain themselves by sea-mammal hunting and by fishing; others, like the Reindeer Tungus, the Chukchi, the Koryak, and the Samoyed, depend on combinations of reindeer herding, fishing, and a variety of hunting. Dogs are eaten, sacrificed, and play roles as guards, herders, and haulers. Emphasis is on cooperating households, and communities are rarely large. Most striking is the belief in spirits, which all of them share. Good luck charms, animal sacrifices, and belief in auspicious or malevolent symbols are prevalent. Shamanism is the practice of contacting and controlling the supernatural through ritual, in which drumming and trance are essential religious techniques. Dreams are especially important as statements of reality, and both dreaming and the interpretation of dreams have much to do with a sense of a teeming sentient world and what is manifest in the spirit cosmos. Much of the folklore is based on tales and incidents of the hunt; hospitality is widely practiced. Archeology indicates that this way of life has endured in Asia since the Pleistocene.

To the south, a second way of life, that of Central Asia, marks the cultural landscape from the puszta of Hungary to the plains of Manchuria. It is a vast corridor of grasslands, mountain chains, plateaus, deserts, and upland forests. Here the basic way of life is pastoralism, whether the transhumant kind of seasonal moves upland and lowland, or the migratory kind along stipulated routes from region to region. This is the country of the horse, camel, goat, and sheep. In the uplands, such as the Tibetan plateau, the yak is the basic herd animal. Agriculture is possible throughout most of the region, but it tends to belong to sedentary populations resident in oases or river valleys. Exchange of the products of herding—hide, hair, meat, and raw materials—for agricultural produce and manufactured goods has kept sedentary and pastoral Central Asia in harmony during much of its history. Commerce throughout Central Asia has been a source of revenue, and payment for the protection of caravans has been a natural course of events.

In Central Asian social organization, women are regarded as property. Bride price, groom service, and dowry are significant parts of the economic determinants for marriage. Patrilineal household lineages leading to larger social units grouped into sodalities are commonplace. Tribalism often maintained by charismatic leadership leads sometimes to groupings of tribes. These groupings come about when pastoral lands are threatened by outsiders, when surpluses of animal stock exist, or when pasturage is scarce and the need acute for concerted action to find other resources. Successful pastoralism is no simple matter of moving herds about according to season. It requires a keen understand-

Bukhara draws much of its water from a large, ancient pool in front of the citadel. The pool is a place to gather and socialize. (1896)

208

The Yakut originally migrated to Siberia from Central Asia and have retained many of their traditions. Their language is related to the Turkic languages of the Near East and Russia. Unlike most Siberian groups who rely on the reindeer, the Yakut place great value on their small, shaggy horses. (Waldemar Jochelson, c. 1900)

ing of water and soil resources, but above all of the durability of the herds. There are just so many miles per day that the herd can reasonably cover, just so much food and water available. There are times of the year when the household groups must scatter over the landscape, other times when concentration is necessary. Raiding is a respected way of winning extra wealth, enhancing herds, and acquiring women. Considerable prestige is obtained by the successful raider, and feats of horsemanship, combat, and general derring-do are celebrated in song and story. Raiding can be offset only by vigilance, and nomadic encampments are set up with that in mind.

Religion has a strong shamanistic element, but Central Asian beliefs include vaguely conceived creator-deities and pantheons that classify the natural features of the landscape. Household, clan, and tribal lineages may have totemic origins. Genghis Khan, for example, is said to have been of a lineage originating in the mating of a deer and a wolf. The Seljuk Turks conquered the West Turkestan region in the eighth century A.D., led by a legendary gray wolf. As in northern Asia, charm, amulet, and prophecy play roles in determining luck and the auspicious thing to do, such as offering hospitality to the stranger or lone traveler. In such cases there is a prescribed code of behavior. For example, the typical pastoral nomadic house is circular and dome-shaped and it is constructed of a light wooden frame overlain by a felt cover. These yurt houses break down and are portable. In these houses there is a central place serving religious purposes, and a section for women and for men with a central fire as pivot. Guests usually are placed in honored positions relative to the male section, the hearth, and the shrine. Hospitality provides for survival, for the exchange of news, and for the mystique of successful travel in a world not without its hazards.

Historically, the Huns, Mongols, Turks, Aryans, Scythians, Sarmatians, and Ephal-

Mongol women had a great deal more independence than Chinese women, and some were as skilled at horseback riding as men. Here, women from northern Mongolia wear the elaborate headdress that is typical of their tribe. (Yvette Borup Andrews, 1918)

ites, all of whom were originally pastoral nomads, have played important roles in drastically influencing old civilized states to the south, east, or west of their traditional homelands. This has caused a number of historians to consider pastoral life as unstable and subject to the vagaries of climate cycles. Recent study of the subject demonstrates that pastoral life is far from unstable. In fact the capability of the pastoralist to move about makes him less vulnerable to the problems of climate faced by the village farmer. Rather than the shrinkage of herds due to climatic problems, it is often the prosperity of the pastoralist that causes the desire to raid. Such reasons are when the herds are too large to guard and, because of their size, consume too much of the available grass and water; when revenge for being raided is a factor; and when the desire to increase pasturage to support the augmented herds leads to ambitious attempts to increase support by alliances and with the promise of a share in the fruits of a successful incursion on others' territory. Usually there is little loss of life on these raids, for the intentions are less to destroy than to seize, and the alliances last only so long as success in economic advantage is maintained. To this degree instabilities exist, but they are expected and normal to tribal life. There are occasions, however, where charismatic leadership, meeting more and more success in forming alliances and sustaining them successfully in raiding, can create pastoral nomadic states that are capable of making war on the always vulnerable sedentary states with which they are in contact. Such was the case with the Seljuk Turks in Iran, with the Mongols in the thirteenth century, with the Manchus in the seventeenth century, and to some extent with the Huns under Attila, and with the Indo-Aryans much earlier. But these pastoral nomadic states did not last long, their unity being dependent too much on leadership charisma and successful conquest. Many formerly pastoral nomadic

The Mongolian yurt is beautifully adapted to the harsh climate of the Gobi Desert and to the Mongol way of life. The yurt is constructed of a covering of felt over a collapsible framework of wooden rods, and is portable, warm, and windproof. The yurt interior usually has a small altar bearing a picture of Buddha, a hearth, and a few boxes and chests. The seat of honor was always at the back of the yurt. (J.B. Shackelford, 1922)

The nomadic Mongols reckoned wealth in terms of sheep, ponies, cattle, camels, and goats. Sheep were important because they provided wool for making the felt covering for the yurt, the typical Mongol dwelling, in the background. (J.B. Shackelford, 1928)

groups settled into sedentary, or even urban, life and played major roles in subsequent histories of the regions in which they remained, such as the Uzbeks of Samarkand, the Turkmen of Merv, the Manchus of China, the Hazara of Afghanistan, and the Seljuk-Ottomans of Anatolia. Even today there is pride taken in the derring-do of the old pastoral nomadic life. One hears it in the folk songs and poetry. There is little doubt that in the Soviet Union today the memory of a once freer life is a cohesive factor in the Central Asian republics like those of the Turkmen, Uzbek, Kazakh, and Kirghiz, in spite of the "obvious benefits" of sedentary life.

Central Asian people have interdigitated into Siberia where the Turkic-speaking Ya-kut, for example, form one of the most prosperous of Siberian aboriginal groups. They adapted the horse to Siberia, and their ritual consumption of kumiss, or fermented mare's milk, with the concurrent celebration of the deities of the sky and earth, emphasizes their Central Asian origins. This is also true of the Buriat Mongols of Transbaikalia, who, in spite of a Tibetan Buddhist veneer, still speak of *tengri*, a non-Buddhist Lord of Heaven familiar in the days of Genghis Khan.

The states and peoples generally to the south of Central Asia are Turkey, Iran, Afghanistan, Baluchistan, Kashmir, Nepal, Sikkim, Tibet, Bhutan, the native states of Burma, Thailand, Cambodia, Laos, Vietnam, and Korea, and the Caucasian regions including Georgia and Armenia. All of these countries and culture regions tend to combine long indigenous cultural uniquenesses with integrations or combinations with alien cultural influences or even people. But of course there are differences in kind. Korea, for example, has been influenced by a long Siberian tradition, which includes such things as shamanism, dog-eating, and face-painting; it has a Central Asian tie in its polysyllabic language, which may eventually relate to Ural-Altaic or Mongol; China has been the strongest influence, contributing Buddhism (with Tibet), Confucianism, much invention, and the written language; Japan has in recent years also made its contribution with elements of modernization. Yet there is a clear Korean culture, which is derived from a long independent history of integration and indigenous growth. This can be said also of Armenia, the oldest Christian state in Asia and thus in the world. Whereas Korea is a bridgeland between China, Japan, and Siberia, Armenia is not in the mainstream of contact between major cultural regions. It is more isolated than Korea, yet, as with other Caucasian areas, it has been the recipient of powerful outside influences from the Islamic Near East, Iran, and the Ukraine. In costume, much decorative art, and vocabulary, Armenia shows these influences, yet its integrity as a unique people remains to this day. The traditional Armenian ethos has been preserved by the power of the Armenian Church which insured its survival by ritual and example.

Turkey is a mountainous country and a strategic one for it is a bridgeland like Korea. On its western perimeter, the Ionian Greeks created an integrated Eurasian way of life prior to the birth of classical Greece, in which the pre-Socratic philosophers probed the

(text continued on page 225)

A demon or masked dancer, a favorite subject, is depicted in this nineteenth-century wood carving from Burma. Height: 40 inches

OPPOSITE:

This traditional woman's costume is from the Ch'uan Miao tribe living on the Szechuan-Yunnan border. The Miao are not ethnic Chinese although their dress and its ornamentation show some influence of Chinese culture. The basketry hat is plaited with thread to resemble hair, and, like the dress, is decorated with the distinctive cross-stitch embroidery that is typical of the Chu'an Miao groups of Southeast Asia.

A pwe, *the traditional theater of Burma, is depicted on this exceptionally fine silver teapot. Height: 7 inches*

The Goldi, a Siberian tribe living on the lower reaches of the Amur River, made various charms out of wood and considered the bear to be a particularly powerful spirit. This bear charm was used to relieve rheumatism. Height: 21 inches

OPPOSITE:

Gautama Buddha founded the Buddhist faith in India around 500 B.C. When Buddhism spread from India to Southeast Asia, Gautama became a common image in Southeast Asian art. This statue belongs to a well-known fifteenth-century Thai style, centered at the northern capital of Chiang Mai. The Buddha is shown seated with the right hand performing the gesture of "calling the earth to witness," a reference to the event following his enlightenment when the Earth Goddess arose at his touch and drowned the troops of the Demon Mara, who was attempting to impede the Buddha's spiritual progress. On the modern base is inscribed in Thai: "Presented to Henry H. Getty by His Royal Highness Prince Damrong of Siam." Height: 27½ inches

This ivory pipe with bears, seals, and walruses was made by the Maritime Koryak. Length: 4¼ inches

OPPOSITE:

The Siberian Yakut kumiss *festival annually invoked the good will of the gods. During the ceremony, a little kumiss (fermented mare's milk), was poured on the ground from a wooden kumiss vessel, shown here, as a gift to the gods, and the rest was drunk with much dancing and celebration. During the ceremony, the chief shaman threw the kumiss ladle (not shown) into the air; if it landed bowl up, it meant the gods would confer success and prosperity on the people. Height: 23½ inches*

Unlike most Siberian tribes that depended on herds of reindeer, Yakut wealth centered around horses and cattle. This elaborate wood and silver saddle reflects the importance of the horse. It also shows the Central Asian roots of the Yakut people. Height: 12¼ inches

This fine coat from the Goldi tribe is made entirely of embroidered, overlayed salmon skin. The Goldi subsisted primarily on salmon and sea mammals, and are sometimes referred to by the Russians as the "Fishskin Tatars" because of their salmon-skin clothing. Length: 110½ inches

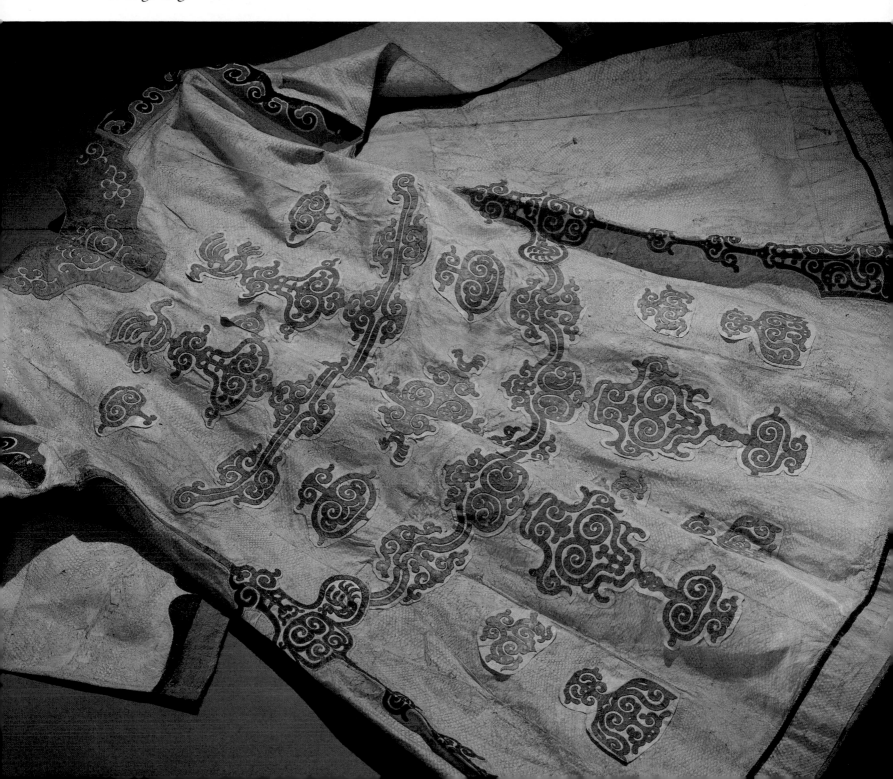

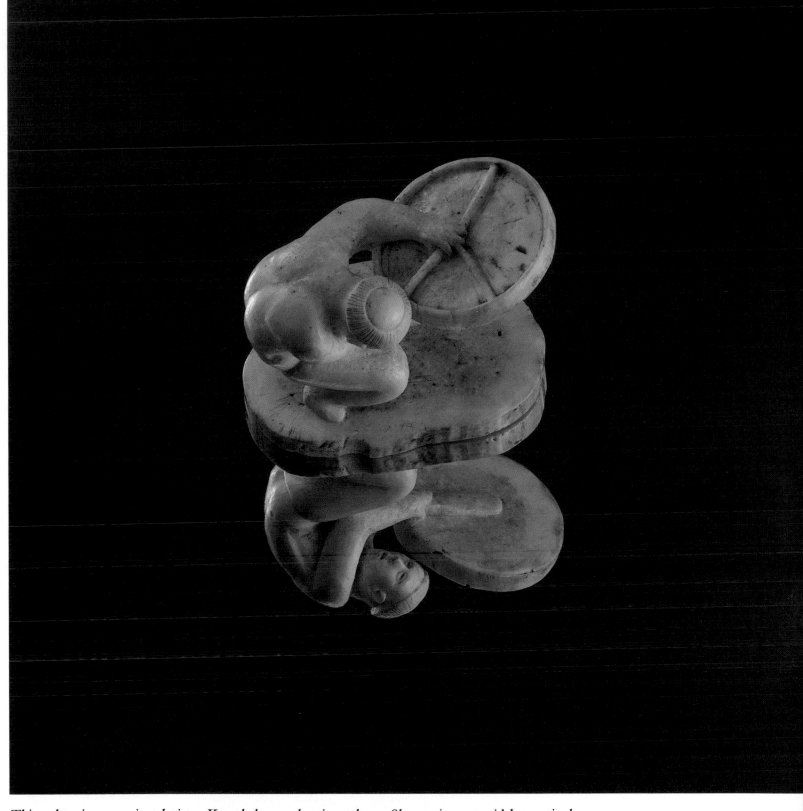

This walrus-ivory carving depicts a Koryak shaman beating a drum. Shamanism was widely practiced among the aboriginal cultures of Siberia. When a person fell ill, it meant an evil spirit had stolen his soul and a shaman was called in to recapture it. The shaman often beat a drum to put himself into a trance, in which he could track down and fight the evil spirit and bring back the soul. Shamans were sometimes chained while in a trance to prevent the evil spirit from stealing them away as well. Height: 2½ inches

OPPOSITE:

This piece of birchbark covered with designs is a love letter written in pictographs by a Siberian Yukaghir girl in the late nineteenth century. The letter tells the story of an important man who is leaving his house. Two girls are infatuated with him, but his status is too high so they return to their boyfriends. One couple has a tenuous relationship, the other a strong and enduring one. Primitive techniques of pictorial writing such as this are thought to be similar to early precursors of true writing. Height: 5½ inches

In an area where survival was uncertain, charms were an integral part of Siberian belief. The wooden fireboard, used to create fire with a bow and drill, was also revered as one of the principal household charms of the Chukchi and some other Siberian peoples. It was thought of as guardian of the vital reindeer herds. The drill holes are called the "eyes" of the fireboard, and the squeak of drilling its "voice." Height: 22 inches

(*text continued from page 212*)

known world with a rationality rooted in Asian learning and European pragmatism. The Trojan wars were fought there, and the Greek army under Xenophon reached the Black Sea and completed the Anabasis there. Lydia, in west-central Anatolia, produced the world's first coinage, while the world's first historian, Herodotus, was born in Halicarnassus. For centuries Anatolia was a refuge region and a bridgeland where myriad people found their home: Paul of Tarsus, the Byzantines, the Ottoman Turks who conquered the Near East and ruled it until World War II, all derived their energies from the control of the region. But Anatolia is too poor in resources to sustain great numbers of people and all those who ruled it have had to control the hinterlands; it is the basic problem of modern Turkey. Yet that very outward necessity gives the people of the peninsula the energy to develop what they do have, integrating what other cultures have offered.

Iran is a substantive example of this phenomenon of indigenous cultural energy combined with powerful outside influences. The whole western part of Iran is occupied by largely non-Persian peoples: Kurds, Bakhtiari, Lurs, Kashgai. In Khuzistan are Arabs, in the northwest Azerbaijani, in the northeast Turkmen, while Baluch live in the southeast. The old Iranian stock is Tajik, and the language of the Persians is Indo-European. The history of Iran demonstrates that that rugged region is best ruled by a central power capable of controlling the enormously varied ethnic entities living there. As early as the Achaemenid Persian Empire, the division of Iran along ethnic lines under a powerful overall ruler was the traditional polity. What was true then was true under the Parthians, the Sassanians, and all the Iranian, Turkish, and Mongol dynasties that followed. Iranians were very conscious of strength. The Iranian male joined athletic clubs or watched exhibitions of strength: club-twirling, weight-lifting, and wrestling were favorite pastimes. Rulers who destroyed opposition were respected, and unity of diverse peoples under a powerful ruler was an Iranian trait.

Yet this physical aspect of Iranian life has to be balanced with the gentling effect of a respect for accomplishment of other kinds. Islam in Iran is not the Islam of other nations. It is Shia and recognizes Imamship. Shia has its fanatic side, but it also has its unorthodoxy. To a very real extent Shia is an Iranian creation and within it arts such as miniature painting, landscape gardening, rug-weaving, and fine metallurgy have flourished as nowhere else in Western Asia. It is no coincidence that the great Moghul cities of India owe their most beautiful monuments to Persian artisans. In literature, the splendors of the *Shah-nameh* of Firdausi, the lyric profundities of Hafiz, Sadi, and Omar, far excel almost all other such efforts in the Islamic world. The accomplishments of Persia are renowned throughout Asia. The famous Shōsōin museum in Nara, Japan, contains a vast collection of the arts and crafts of Asia which reached Japan in the eighth century A.D. In it are substantive representations of the Persian artist.

Iran best represents the role of trade east and west in developing a hybrid cultural ethos outside the civilized stabilities described in early chapters. The old cities, Isfahan, Teheran, Mashhad, Merv, Bukhara, Samarkand, Tashkent, Herat, Kandahar, Multan and eastward, are for the most part Iranian in character. This is represented not only in architecture but by the use of Persian as a lingua franca. "All roads lead to Isfahan" is a true saying and demonstrative of the bridgeland character of this vital country, which is central to the interrelationships of the Caucasus, the Near East, Central Asia, and the Indo-Pakistan subcontinent.

Afghanistan is a new, old state. In a smaller fashion, it is similar to Iran, to which it largely owes its cultural character. But it is closer to the Indo-Pakistan subcontinent, and the relationships of its Pushtu-speaking Pathan majority are to the Khyber and the northwest frontier of Pakistan. It is a mountainous, closed land, hybrid in population, and its varied ethnic groups are fiercely independent. In this, they are no different from the peoples of the Caucasus or the Kham tribesmen of eastern Tibet. But there is something of a difference, for nature has not been good to the Afghans. The mountains are barren, the deserts broad, and even the fertile zones are productive only with the hardest work. Irrigation is essential in much of the land. The *khanat* or *karez*, the underground system of water-tapping, and the irrigation canal are manifest everywhere. The Pathan takes pride in his fields and begs God to help maintain them in the face of adversity. Men wear flowers in their hair and bullets in slings across their chests. They boast of familial and

Several Turkomans (identified by their sheepskin headdress) take tea (chai) in Bukhara. The men of Bukhara wear colorful robes, especially on Friday, the Muslim holy day, when they are clothed in spotless white turbans and traditional robes of rich purples, blues, pinks, yellows, and greens. Color on a Muslim woman, however, would be frowned upon; most wear the traditional horsehair veils and gray cloaks. (1896)

These women and boys are wearing kolas, *a traditional headcovering in Central Asia and the Near East. (J. L. Clark, 1920s)*

clan affiliations, wear long hair, and are the most tenacious fighters in the world. Expansive in hospitality, fanatic in their defense of what is theirs, they are a great paradox for the Westerner. They are, I suspect, in one people the graphic illustration of all that is bad and good in mankind. Compulsive competitors, they drive madly the buses and trucks that replace the caravans of old. Consequently, the rate of highway accidents due to overspeeding and daredevil acts is very high in both Afghanistan and Pakistan.

What is true of the Pathan is also true generally for the Baluch. But the Baluch have tended more to pastoralism than the Pathan, and their pride in the land is more in terms of pasture than plot. Baluchistan involves also a Dravidian language group, the Brahui, who form the backbone of the Baluchistan state of Kalat, not recognized in today's politics but supremely important for its unity in the mountainous desert lands of eastern Baluchistan. Baluchistan is one of the Asian lands that is vast in area, but its aridity makes it generally inhospitable to sedentary life. Consequently it is sparsely inhabited. Most of the population practices transhumance, but there is a smaller percentage who maintain themselves on the limited agricultural land the year around. Basically, the country is a place of the nomad; the very name "Baluch" means "wanderer." It is probably the hottest land on earth with temperatures averaging 97 degrees the year over and in summer reading over 150 degrees amid the bare rocks of the thirsty, empty valleys. Combine this with the violent dust winds, and one can understand the reason for the saying: "Oh, God, if you already had hell why did you make Baluchistan!" Yet for all its physical hazards the Baluch-Brahui are as adapted as Eskimos in the Arctic. In song, legend, and story, they recount the courage it takes to live in Baluchistan, of tribal raiding and deeds of conquest, of magic and far places, and of their ultimate devotion to their land.

In both Pathan and Baluch we have clear examples of the capability of man to adapt to extremes of climate and landscape. The fact that their life is marked by aggressiveness

A Mongol lama wears a hat of sheep's wool. Buddhism is the prevalent religion of Mongolia, and the countryside is dotted with monasteries that were protected and served by feudal princes who held sway over various regions. Almost every Mongol family would raise at least one boy for the celibate life of a monk; up to one third of the male population of Mongolia were lamas. (Yvette Borup Andrews, 1919)

and that they trace their tribal lineages back to famous warriors is symptomatic of the obvious fact that in these borderlands of Iran and India the aggressive survive and "the meek are slaves or dead."

It is a different world entirely when one travels along the inner borders of the Indo-Pakistan subcontinent, moving eastward from the borders of Kafiristan and Kashmir—the last home of ancient paganism within the Muslim sphere of the borderland country: Ladakh, Nepal, Sikkim, and Bhutan. In this mountain region the valleys are broad and rivers meander however so slightly; soil is good and the local peasantry tills it mightily; elsewhere terracing and patching occur, often at considerable heights. For the rest, there are pastoral nomads amid the hills, but pastoralism is generally less important than agriculture as an economic enterprise, for only goats, sheep, and yaks can profit from high pasturage. Great distances, many of them vertical, must necessarily be covered for grazing purposes and handicap the successful development of large flocks of sheep and goats. Local pastoralism in places like Kashmir, however, has made possible the development of long goat hair and sheep wool, which are celebrated the world over for their fineness.

There are few cities in these lands. The ones that exist are basically commercial, administrative, or religious centers, and one or two such places within national borders suffice. The village and the farm are the hallmarks of settlement in this Himalayan country. Barley, the most hardy of the cereal crops, is a staple, but rice, millet, and wheat are important particularly in the lower valleys. These crops, plus truck gardening and horticulture in much of the cultivable areas, give a rich diversity to the diet that has the potential of making these people among the healthiest in the world. The bitter cold of upland winters, however, plus cultural habits that play their part in sustaining attitudes have worked against this potential.

The organization of society is usually threefold: aristocracy, farmers most of whom are peasants, and the pastoral nomads. In addition, there are subgroups, such as the Lepchas of Sikkim, who tend to avoid involvement in the affairs of the larger group and are essentially self-effacing. Trade across the difficult passes that separate the settled areas may be carried on by nonindigenous folk such as Tibetans, Sikhs, and Hindus. This trade has created a regular network of roads over which are carried the commodities important from region to region: salt, sugar, silk, coral, turquoise, leather, silver, incense, brass objects, and dried fruits—an exotic cargo that has helped to make the bazaars of the whole region famous.

Historically, the relationship between India and Tibet, and more remotely China, has been of the greatest influence. It appears that these regions were only sparsely populated in their main centers until around A.D. 500 when growing numbers of inner-Asian and south-Asian people found their way there. The way of life was essentially sedentary village farming and the religion was Tibetan Buddhism. But in Kashmir and Nepal, Islam and Hinduism have been far more prevalent in more recent times.

Ideologically, and to a very real extent culturally, Tibet has had the greatest influence. It is a high plateau country, situated above 12,000 feet, surrounded on all sides by very high mountains, and with many lakes and rivers. Major settlement is in the south and east, close to the borderland states where the Tsang-po (later the Brahmaputra) River waters lowland tracts of fertile soil. Here is Lhasa, the capital of Tibet, as well as the monastery town Shigatse, which lies on the highroad to Sikkim and India. It is a remote, difficult region. Pastoral nomads dependent on the yak live in symbiosis with Tibetan farmers in the lowlands, exchanging hides, hair, and felt for cereal crops and manufactured goods. Traditionally, most of the farmers have some relationship to local monasteries, receiving aspects of worship and manufactured objects of daily use in return for barley and truck-garden products. Most farming families have a son, who is a celibate monk in a monastery. Only in towns such as Lhasa, seat of the Dalai Lama, the traditional ruler of Tibet, is there an aristocracy. Trade and the hereditary possession of land have made the aristocracy possible, and from this group has come the secular bureaucracy of the country. All this changed with the Communist Chinese take-over in 1959.

Tibet and its borderlands have been a source of considerable fascination for the Westerner. Tibetan Buddhism, which is historically an amalgam of local animism (Pön) with Mahayana and Tantric Buddhism, as well as a strong influx of Hinduism, has so many facets that no one of them can truly be said to represent the faith. It is perfectly possible to study Tibetan Buddhism in terms of the highest esoterism or as a pantheistic creed. It has shamanistic elements and elements of the highest rationality, and has been accredited with acts of incredible magic and with significant degrees of skepticism. The terror of its *dharmapala* conceptions contrasts with the sublimeness of its Taras, Avalokitesvaras, and the Buddhas themselves. The monotonous, often seemingly meaningless repetition of much textual ritual forms a background to the lively, heartfelt song-poems of the great Tibetan saint Milarepa:

In the solitary dwelling of Byan-cub-rdzon
Above, there stands the high white glacier of the mighty gods.
Passing below are many faithful patrons.
Behind me is a hill cut off by a white silk curtain;
Before me, a forest which grants every wish.
On the lotus of pleasing scent,
The insects are humming.
On the shores of the ponds and pools,
The water birds turn their necks to see.
On the wide branches of the wish-granting trees,
Assemblages of beauteous birds are singing.
The cool breezes carry fragrances,
And dancing gestures are made by the branches of the trees.

(THE 100,000 SONGS OF MILAREPA,
translated by A. K. Gordon.
Charles E. Tuttle, Rutland, Vermont.)

The institution of the Dalai Lama, whereby a new ruler is chosen when the old one dies on the basis of stigmata that indicate reincarnation, confirms the powerful influence of the Hindu karma—the cycle of rebirths. The difference is, of course, that the Dalai Lama's reincarnations are those of a bodhisattva: purposeful rebirths for the benefit of man. This is generally true in Tibet, Sikkim, Bhutan, Ladakh, and much of Nepal. Much of authority in the high borderlands is religious in nature, and much of law is the pragmatic and workable law of indigenous morality expressed in religion. It is a generally nonviolent region. Women have property rights and are generally equal to men, with whom they work as partners. Children are much loved and laughter comes easily. Marriage is a business affair, where the gain or loss of property, which is involved necessarily as a mark of inheritance, has to be seriously considered in any matrimonial affair. Kindness to strangers and a genuine sense of piety to the faith are characteristic of most of the different people. Mountaineers, who have attempted Himalayan heights supported, indeed led, by the Sherpas, universally return to comment on their reliability, friendship, and good humor. British officers, who led Gurkha regiments in World War II, had nothing but praise for their courage and good spirits. It is strange that this mixture of Nepalese volunteers for the military, many of whom are Buddhists, should have the reputation of being preeminent among the world's fighting units.

It is very easy to wax eloquent about these high borderland people. One can also describe the dirt, high infant mortality, venereal disease, and the dogged animistic beliefs that pervade the whole region and often interfere with proper medical treatment, but in the scheme of things there can be no judgment. For he who judges must stand somewhere, and I do not know anyone who can stand higher physically and ethically than the people of the high borderlands. Given their Buddhist faith and their marvelous ability to function high above sea level, they have achieved a remarkable level of human happiness.

Mainland Southeast Asia includes the subcontinental frontiers of Burma, the Shan

A Tibetan monk holds a prayer wheel and rosary. The prayer wheel, used by Tibetan Buddhists, is a metal cylinder with rolls of finely printed prayers inside it. Each rotation about the stick counts as one repetition of all the prayers inside the cylinder. (W.J. Morden, 1920s)

The Black Hat Dance (cham) *was one of many dance-dramas performed by monks in Tibet during the New Year celebrations. The monks are holding (from left): a lasso to catch the fleeing demon, a chain to bind him, a skeleton club to deal him the death blow, and a skull to catch the demon's precious blood. The objects in this photograph were acquired by the photographer and given to the American Museum of Natural History; the mask on the far right is pictured on page 34. (Rev. H.B. Marx, c. 1920)*

A dancer at the birthday party of the king of Cambodia exhibits her skill. This is probably one of the royal Khmer palace dancers who perform for the king and on special occasions. Although masked men perform the most formal classical dances, women without masks dance a related form known as the lakon. Lakon *dances are based on local folklore and mythology and usually tell a story. The royal dancers are garbed in costumes of brocade and wear crowns of beaten gold set with diamonds. (W.J. Morden, 1920s)*

Reflected in the moat surrounding the Mandalay palace constructed by King Mindon in 1857 is one of the twelve gates decorated by a pyatthat, or pavilion of wood. (Epstein, recent)

232

states, parts of southeastern China, Thailand, Malaya, Cambodia, Laos, and the old states of Vietnam: Annam, Cochin, and Tonkin. This is also a mountainous region where on the slopes, upland valleys, and plateaus exist a bewildering variety of tribal people, most of whom practice slash-and-burn agriculture and who trade the products of their jungled slopes with the people of the lowlands. A strict division between the territories of the tribal people and those of the lowlands has been a tradition for as far back as records go. In recent years departure from this tradition, because of modernization, has been the cause of considerable conflict. This is a hot, monsoonal region for the most part, and the lush vegetation of the jungle marks it, as the Himalayan snows mark the high borderlands.

The mountains trend north-south and, coupled with the regularity of rainfall, large rivers are formed whose deltas are enormous. Southeast Asia has been known as the rice bowl of Asia because of the great fertility of these delta "gardens." It is one of the world's greatest tragedies that this region now has starving people.

Agriculture may well have started indigenously in Southeast Asia with the early domestication of such plants as beans, peas, and cucumbers, perhaps around 8000 B.C. There is something of an academic controversy as to whether rice cultivation began in Southeast Asia and diffused to India and China, or whether it was the reverse. The inability of archeologists to work systematically in such places as Burma, Vietnam, and Bangladesh has prevented the accumulation of any substantive evidence to confirm one theory or the other. But there is a tantalizing suggestion that Southeast Asia had priority, along with the development of bark cloth, the cultivation of black pepper, and even the domestication of the water buffalo.

Whatever the priorities, good evidence in the Chinese records shows that wet rice agriculture was practiced in Tonkin as early as the middle of the first millennium B.C. Bronze-working was already known for perhaps a thousand years prior to this time. With the Han dynasty's imperial role, Chinese expansion into Tonkin occurred, bringing with it Chinese innovation in crafts, in bronze-work, and possibly in social organization. The evidence is that the lowlands of Tonkin and the coastal east were characterized by village settlements on whom the Confucian system may have had an increasingly strong influence.

The broad delta regions of Burma, Thailand, Cambodia, and central Vietnam were apparently settled by the time of Christ by sedentary village farmers emphasizing wet rice cultivation. Characteristic of Southeast Asia is the general movement from north to south of various peoples, most of whom followed the river valleys. There has also been some movement laterally of local hill people into these valleys as well. The settlements appear to have been scattered and to some degree isolated from one another although connections along the great interior waterways must have been fairly easy. The specific settled areas are unknown to us, but some among them were certainly by the shores of the Tonle Sap (Great Lake) of Cambodia and near the shores of the Irrawaddy, Mekong, and Menam rivers, at places where later important population centers were to spring up. These settlements were probably headed by chiefs, who were capable of mustering the population for land clearance, irrigation, and the community's defense. Although populations could not have been large, aggressive attitudes existed between settlements and with hill people, which warranted defensive measures.

South Indian civilization established by the Tamils had reached a considerable height by the time of Christ, while at the same time Bengal was ruled by princes of Indo-Aryan origin. It may well be that the famous Indian epic, the *Ramayana*, which tells of travels from the Bengal region (or its equivalent) to Ceylon, was of this time. A Roman seaport has been found at Arikamedo, near Pondicherry, and a first century A.D. Pompeian lamp has been recovered at Chiang Mai in northern Thailand. All this adds up to the fact that Indian traders or middlemen, like the ancestral Malays, were crossing the Bay of Bengal to Southeast Asia. With them came priests, adventurers, scribes, and savants of one kind or another. This started the process of Indianization, which was to produce some of the most important monuments in the world as a consequence of great Southeast Asian monarchies. Whatever the Indian influence, however, it was the indigenous culture that left its distinct stamp.

Animism has been mentioned before and it must be reiterated in the context of Southeast Asia. In the West, we objectify in order to understand. Supposing you have a pet that you love very much, and supposing it is hurt or becomes ill. You take your pet to the veterinarian and you may be quite dismayed to have him treat it simply as an animal, an object on which he can practice his trade. If the pet dies, it becomes a statistic to him, not the loss of a friend. The doctor has turned the subject into an object. Much of the

A hand-dug shaft 150 to 250 feet deep was used to recover oil in Burma in the nineteenth and early twentieth centuries. To get the oil, a man was lowered at the end of a rope to the bottom of the pit, where he would scoop oil in a bucket before being raised, each "dive" lasting about fifteen to twenty minutes. In this photograph of a well at Yenanyaung, the man in the well has an air hose (right) leading to a kerosene tin over his head to protect him from fumes and falling earth. Even after boring for oil was introduced in Burma in 1887 (using American cable rigs, visible in background), the hand-dug shafts remained in use. (W.J. Morden, 1920s)

In South Okkalapa, near Rangoon, the Melamu Buddha holds an alms bowl. Beside him in the trees he is flanked by chinthes, *or mythical lions. In addition to Buddhist shrines and images, Rangoon has places of worship for Muslims, Hindus, Parsis, and Christians.*

problem of human engineering in the world today is caused by governments or authorites treating human beings as objects rather than as mothers, fathers, sisters, or loved ones. It is the fatal flaw of Western man's science, for carried to its limits it denies the existence of the gods.

But in Southeast Asia all life exists, all things function because there is a spirit energy, however it is called. This energy can be particular—as what makes the arm move—or general, as the consciousness of rice's nutritional value. Remove this energy and you have death, illness, or famine. In addition to the energy apparent in sentient things, gods and spirits function in a variety of ways to affect man and nature. Each of these has his own energy and rites are performed to make this energy function. Moreover, mountains, stars, sun, moon, and rivers radiate their special energies, which in turn can influence events. Horoscope-reading is man's way of determining these influences. Clearly the Southeast Asian's animism not only classifies the world by function but it structures it also. For there are obviously planes of existence: the world of animals, of spirits, of gods, of evil, and of human beings. Each of these planes has its own dimension and the occupants behave according to their own rules, character, and role. Thus the village farmer cultivates according to the seasons, just as the god of the monsoon brings rain. The ancient Asian idea of worlds upon worlds in a cosmos in which all phenomena are encompassed is given vivid expression in Southeast Asia as a means of comprehending what is mathematically incomprehensible and of establishing cause for each effect. Bad luck, disease, love, or a good crop are the consequences of a relationship between men

Angkor Wat in Cambodia is a magnificent temple complex that was built by Suryavarman II in the twelfth century. The complex is adorned with relief carvings and statuary depicting Hindu and Buddhist subjects and scenes of the royal court and army. The guardian figure shown here is one of many lining the entrance route to this great architectural monument. (Murphy, recent)

and spirits where each has crossed the perimeters of the given realm by misbehavior or remains within and fulfills the laws of that realm with resultant profit. Human existence, then, is influenced by supernatural forces, which must be controlled by ritual, rite, amulet, prayer, and sacrifice.

This ideology was assumed to be paramount in Southeast Asia when the Indian traders and their retinue came there. Between the second and the ninth centuries, the process of Indianization brought the popular Hindu gods and forms of Buddhism. But whatever the influence of these religions, conversion from the animistic beliefs did not generally occur. What did happen was the development of a special form of kingship.

In ancient Egypt, the pharaoh was regarded in the Old Kingdom as a god, even as the sun god Re. His divinity was directly related to the correlation that Egypt's prosperity owed to the pharaoh's presence in the midst of the people. So long as the land prospered, so long was the pharaoh's status as god unimpaired. The Southeast Asian monarchies that came into power were in many ways similar. The kings of Angkor, near the Tonle Sap, were regarded as incarnations of certain Hindu gods—Siva and Vishnu—while those in the Burma region may have claimed to be bodhisattvas or their equivalent.

If you believe that the world is square, where is its center? For the classical civilizations of Angkor and Pagan (Burma) the center of the world was where the seat of manifest power was located—the city of the king. The city itself was laid out as a microcosm of the cosmos, an orderly unity surrounding the seat of the divine royal energy, perhaps the lingam of Siva or a sacred relic of the Buddha. The king was a *devaraja* (god-king) in one form or another, and he retained his power so long as victory in war and the creation of architectural wonders were maintained. Royal power was in essence the expression of kingship, and the spirit world's obedience to royal will was emulated in the obedience of human beings to that same will. With that obedience the *devaraja* could create the cosmos in stone, as in the wondrous cities of Angkor and Pagan . . . now in ruins.

The Tai-speaking people, who had gradually been moving southward out of China, became more and more dominant after the thirteenth century, and by the fifteenth century brought the demise of the classical civilization of the Khmers, the indigenous people of Thailand-Cambodia. Pagan had fallen to the Mongols in the thirteenth century. Southeast Asia became fragmented politically as the Tai built minor states of their own. Ideologically, it was another matter.

Ceylon, or Sri Lanka, had been a protector of Buddhism during its long persecution in India, and it was there that the earlier form of the faith, Hinayana, was practiced when monks from Southeast Asia came to learn of it as early as the eleventh century. The form that these monks brought to Southeast Asia is known as Theravada (Way of Elders). It

The Maritime Koryak lived in underground dwellings entered by a ladder through the smoke hole in the roof. The photographer describes living in these dwellings: "The smoke, which fills the hut, makes the eyes smart. Walls, ladder, and household utensils are covered with a greasy soot, so that contact with them leaves shining black spots on hands and clothing. The odor of blubber and refuse is almost intolerable. As long as we remained in these dwellings, we could not escape the lice, which we dreaded more than any of the privations of our journey." (Waldemar Jochelson, 1900)

Lacquered horsehair hats were standard male attire in the late nineteenth and early twentieth centuries in Korea. In earlier times these hats had much wider brims, but in the declining Korean economy of the nineteenth century sumptuary laws were passed regulating dress, and from then on hat sizes were restricted to the dimensions of the one shown here. Korean men customarily wore white starched clothing. (Roy Chapman Andrews, 1912)

A group of women walk down a street in Seoul, Korea. In such public places Confucian standards of decorum required very modest attire. In a Confucian society a woman's place was strictly in the home, and relations between the sexes were not a matter for public observation or discussion in polite society. In the home, however, a woman had complete authority over economic and all other family matters.

holds fairly closely to the older Buddhist idea that all living things are part of a chain of causation where one's actions in this life dictate how one will be in the next (karma). If one builds up merit from life to life, it may eventually lead to the end of suffering, which is elemental to living, and thus one achieves a nonsuffering state, Nirvana. Essential to the maintenance of merit is monkhood. Monks teach the Buddhist texts written in Pali, and offer the ordinary man the opportunity to obtain merit by alms-giving and rite, or even the right to temporary monkhood or apprenticeship at some time in life.

One of the most interesting things about the spread of Buddhism in Southeast Asia is that Mahayana, the form of Buddhism that took such a hold in China, Korea, and Japan, was rejected, except in Vietnam where it came from China. Theravada Buddhism can be very esoteric and remote for the average villager. But in Southeast Asia it was accepted from Burma to southern Vietnam, and it is to this day the religion of most of these people. One reason for its favor with the people is the ease with which animistic ideas can be amalgamated with Buddhist cause and effect. Animism shows how bad action can arouse the ire of spirits and condemn the individual to a miserable life. So in the Theravada karma we have a direct parallel: "One is always accountable for one's actions." Thus people have free choice; they can influence their times, expressed in good ways or bad; there is always a consequence. It is therefore normal to find a Buddhist temple in a Southeast Asian village and an animistic shrine—without a basic contradiction between them.

Women in the Vietnamese village are subject to the Confucian ideal of patrilineal descent, resulting from the long Chinese occupation of nearly a thousand years (ended A.D. 939). Interestingly, Vietnamese women can inherit land. Ancestor worship, Chinese-style clothing, and the popularity of certain Chinese gods are symptoms of Chinese influence. Local animism, however, pervades the ideology just as it does in the Theravada areas of Southeast Asia. As the Vietnamese moved southward toward the Mekong Delta, they came into militant contact with the Theravada and other communities that they conquered one by one until they obtained control of the Mekong Delta itself. Their drive was caused in part by the growth of population in Tonkin, which, as in China, is a consequence of a social system where large families are a significant aspect of filial piety.

The contrast between the Burmese, Thai, and Khmer villagers and those of Vietnam is most marked in the patterns of kinship and inheritance. For the Theravada Buddhist, society is based on the nuclear family, not on the large, extended family of the Chinese type. After marriage, the groom and bride remain with the wife's family in many groups. Inheritance of land, which is regarded as female in nature, is through the married daughters. Relations between the sexes is relatively easygoing, and morality is governed by the fear of offending the spirits.

Although the divine city of the past is gone, the respect for shrines and temple-monasteries continues even in the midst of the new Western-style cities. The great divisions of this part of Asia—hill people, the Vietnamese-Chinese-style culture, and the Theravada Thai, Burmese, Laotian, and Khmer—appear to be offset by a common dependence on rice and by a universal belief in the powers of animism. But this does not extend into the government. There are no *devarajas*, the Indian *chakravartin* (world ruler), to relate all these diverse people to a world order, and for this and other reasons Southeast Asia, for all its strong indigenous roots, has rarely had cultural stability and thus the success of its neighbors, China and India. One would think of Southeast Asian civilization as simply the result of borrowing. But when you walk toward the Bayon at Angkor Thom, built some eight hundred years ago at the time of the Magna Carta, and experience the immense power of a silent architecture that is witness to a belief in the

Waldemar Borgoras was one of several Russian anthropologists who went to Siberia and collected for the American Museum of Natural History. He studied a number of aboriginal groups, including the Reindeer Chukchi living on the Kamchatka Peninsula. Like most Siberian and Eskimo groups, the Chukchi love to play, as evidenced by these dancing girls. (Waldemar Borgoras, 1901)

monarchy as the model of the cosmos, you realize the uniqueness of scale, concept, and execution, whatever the borrowing.

The third cultural element, then, of the Asian ethos is a varied one: lands that are isolated and develop their own styles out of the mix of alien influences and of their own indigenous qualities; lands that are bridges to greater cultural traditions and cultivate power to maintain their own cultural identity; and lands with strong indigenous cultural energies, which borrow from outside but shape the borrowing to their own specific uniform style. Stable in their geographic placement, but unstable in their dependence on the energizing cultural flow from outside, these lands of the perimeters of Asia's great traditional stabilities at once preserve old ways with an almost fanatic devotion, and accept the new responsively but with suspicion.

In all, the Asian cultural character has a geographical premise and thus a remarkable diversity within Asia's varied environments. Yet there are four basic, mutually influential unities: the great stable indigenous civilizations; the dynamic borderlands; the great passage pasturelands of the nomadic and oasis peoples of Central Asia; and the far reaches of the Siberian world of Paleo-Asia. Thus history and cultural character in Asia are the consequence of the quality within and the relationships without of these Asian units.

*　　　　*　　　　*　　　　*

The collections made by the American Museum of Natural History in Asia since 1869 are irreplaceable, largely because they are representative of the vanished traditional life of Asian people. The duckbill doll of the Samoyed, the kumiss vessel of the Yakut, the Gujarati brass bowl, the camel gun of the Afghan, the spinning wheel, the Chinese stuffed tiger, and the Japanese cord measurer are no longer made or used. This is symptomatic of what is obvious to everyone: Asia is changing, the world is changing, man's cultural diversity is dying. As Western man boasts of the advances in human technological achievement his civilization has inspired, he denies the possibility that other civilizations may have been on the verge of equally great achievements but in other areas of human accomplishment. We do not have the fruits of the inspired artistic creativity that was just coming into its own in parts of Asia not so long ago; we have lost the evidence of human happiness and the abolition of aggression that some Asian cultures had incorporated into daily life. We are poorer for these losses. It is a comfort for Asians to look back at their traditions as capitalism and communism, the socio-economic philosophies of Western man, drown out the windbells of Buddhism or the flute songs of Tao and Shinto; as the nuclear family of the industrial city wipes out the memory of the respected aged; as the hard-working villager sees the fruits of his labor taken from him by unfeeling government and witnesses the great urban trek that takes his sons from him; as craftsmen lose their motivation to continue age-old techniques in which high skill and delicate movement are requisites taught by father to apprentice son; as mass media manipulate human lives for one purpose or another; as all these and so many more distortions of the human hope for happiness continue. Yet perhaps we of the West will in the end see and learn that there were other ways of life not so long ago, some still struggling to survive, and that these other ways were and are as valid as our own.

AFTERWORD

DOUGLAS J. PRESTON

American Museum of Natural History

WHEN ALBERT S. BICKMORE, a young student of the great zoologist Louis Agassiz, went traveling in Japan and China in 1866 and 1867, he carried with him two things: a Bible and a sketch plan for a museum of natural history in New York City. Upon his return he gave a popular series of lectures in Boston on "The Ainos, or Hairy Men of Saghalien and the Kurile Islands," and shortly thereafter founded the American Museum of Natural History. Thus began the museum's 112-year involvement with the Asian continent.

Most of the photographs and all the artifacts in this book are a result of this interest. When museum scientists, curators, and anthropologists turned to Asia, they saw many different opportunities. Some believed Asia would be the birthplace of the human race, while others looked to Asia as the key to understanding human migrations to the New World. Some saw a chance to study Asian ways of life—so different from our own— which would soon be gone forever. Some thought of Asia as a rich graveyard of dinosaur and mammalian fossils, while others considered the continent as a last frontier, a place of high adventure.

For over a century these people, each with different (and sometimes conflicting) goals, explored the continent and assembled a vast collection of ethnographic and archeo-logical material. In addition to small collecting parties and excursions, the museum sent two great expeditions to Asia—the Jesup and the Central Asiatic—which brought back the major portion of the museum's Asian collections.

The first major expedition to Asia was organized by Morris K. Jesup, a founder of the museum and its third president. He was an archetypal nineteenth-century millionaire.

The sled, clothing, and horse shown in this photograph are typical of the Amur basin, Sakhalin, and the Kuril Islands. There was a cultural similarity among groups in those areas that makes positive identification of this photograph difficult. (probably Berthold Laufer, c. 1900)

Raised by his widowed mother with seven brothers and sisters, Jesup left school at twelve years old to work as an errand boy. By the time he reached his mid-thirties he had made a fortune in railroads and banking. He was a man of large ideas and ambitions who also possessed a quick and inquiring mind and, surprisingly enough, sound scientific reasoning. Jesup subscribed to the theory that America had, in his words, been "peopled by migratory tribes from the Asiatic continent." He wrote: "The opportunities favorable for solving this problem are rapidly disappearing." The opportunities he referred to were the numerous aboriginal tribes living along the rim of the North Pacific, which included the Northwest Coast Indians, the American and Asiatic Eskimo, the Tungus, the Ainu of Japan, and numerous small Siberian tribes.

To settle the question, Jesup organized a series of expeditions lasting from 1897 to 1903 that explored the entire rim of the North Pacific Ocean, from Washington State, the Northwest Coast of British Columbia, and Alaska, to Siberia, Kamchatka, Sakhalin and the Kuril Islands, Hokkaido, Japan, Korea, Manchuria, and China. He placed a young assistant curator in the museum's Department of Anthropology in charge of the expeditions, which were collectively known as the Jesup North Pacific Expedition. His choice was fortuitous: the young curator was Franz Boas, who is today referred to as the father of American anthropology. Although Boas was mildly interested in Jesup's goals, he had a much broader view of what needed to be done. He saw the fragile aboriginal cultures of the North Pacific dying under the influence of the West, and he realized that this would be the last opportunity to study and learn about most of these cultures. His overriding desire was to save every possible thing related to these societies for future study, and, ultimately, for the common heritage of humanity. Boas found three anthropologists to lead expeditions in Asia (Boas himself directed work in North America), a German, Berthold Laufer, and two Russians, Waldemar Jochelson and Waldemar Borgoras.

Boas instructed his men in the field to collect and study everything. Borgoras, in a letter to Boas, gives an idea of the kind of comprehensive work they did in Siberia:

The results of this work are studies of the ethnography and anthropology of the Chukchee and Asiatic Eskimo, and partly of the Kamchadal and of the Pacific Koryak. These studies are illustrated by extensive collections, embracing five thousand ethnographical objects, thirty-three plaster casts of faces, seventy-five skulls and archaeological specimens from abandoned village sites and from graves. Other material obtained includes three hundred tales and traditions; one hundred fifty texts in the Chukchee, Koryak, Kamchadal and Eskimo languages; dictionaries and grammatical sketches of these languages; ninety-five phonographic records, and measurements of eight hundred sixty individuals. I also made a zoological collection and kept a meteorological journal during the whole time of my field-work.

Boas encouraged photography for the study of racial types. Physical anthropology, especially the study of racial features, was an important goal of the expedition since Boas hoped to show a connection between northeastern Asians and Northwest Coast Indians physically as well as culturally. Thousands of individuals were "anthropometrically" measured and photographed from the front, side, and back, resulting in a series of photographs that looked like mug shots. (Although the practice may seem rather strange to us today, it is interesting to note that Albert S. Bickmore insisted that he be photographed from the front, side, and back for an official museum portrait.) Boas and his colleagues had not fully developed the idea of conscious ethnographic documentation using photography, but with cameras along they naturally took photographs of themselves, their camps, and of course the peoples they studied. These ultimately more important and interesting photographs only constitute a small portion of the mass of anthropometric portraits, but they form a very rare collection indeed as they are some of the only photographs of these peoples in existence.

Laufer, Jochelson, and Borgoras studied and traveled separately. Laufer arrived in Vladivostok on June 19, 1898. From there he took a steamer to Sakhalin Island in the Bay of Okhotsk where he remained through the bitter Siberian winter studying the Gilyak, Tungus, and Ainu. He periodically reported his work to Boas, and here is a quote from his dispatch of March 4, 1899:

I did not succeed in obtaining any anthropometric measurements. The people were afraid that they would die at once after submitting to this process. Although I had their confidence, I failed in my efforts in this direction, even after offering them presents which they considered of great value. I succeeded in measuring a single individual, a man of imposing stature, who, after the measurements had been taken, fell prostrate on the floor, the picture of despair, groaning, "Now I am going to die to-morrow!"

I started comparatively late on my journey along the east coast of Saghalin, because I was detained for two months and a half by a severe attack of influenza. As soon as I had sufficiently recovered, I visited one of the Gilyak villages where the people were celebrating one of their bear festivals. I was welcomed with much delight, since I met several of my acquaintances of last summer. For five days I assisted in the ceremonial, and was even permitted to witness the sacrifice of the dog, which is kept secret from the Russians . . . . On New Year's eve I reached my southernmost point on the island. On the following day I took phonographic records of songs, which created the greatest sensation among the Russians as well as among the natives. A young Gilyak woman who sang into the instrument said: "It took me so long to learn this song, and this thing has learned it at once, without making any mistakes. There is surely a man or a spirit in this box which imitates me!" and at the same time she was crying and laughing with excitement.

Jochelson arrived in Siberia a year later, where he was to work with the tribes living above the Arctic Circle. He and his wife, who were both large and imposing Russians, primarily studied the Reindeer Koryak, often under trying conditions. A good indication of the hardships they faced can be seen in this excerpt from one of Jochelson's reports:

Our journey from Kushka, at the mouth of the Gishiga River, to Verkhne-Kolymsk, on the Yassachna River, a tributary of the Kolyma, took fifty-six days—from August 15 until October 9, 1901. We were the first whites to cross the Stanovoi Mountains at this point. This journey was

This view looks up Tiger Canyon in the Gobi Desert, with Boga Bogdo looming in the background. Tserin, the Mongolian guide who led the Central Asiatic Expedition across the Gobi from water hole to water hole, is sitting in the foreground. (J.B. Shackelford, 1925)

This photograph shows the typical courtyard of a caravanserai in Bukhara. Until the city was conquered by the Russians, Bukhara was the capital of the emirate of Bukhara. (1896)

the most difficult one that it was ever my fate to undertake. Bogs, mountain torrents, rocky passes and thick forests combined to hinder our progress. Part of our provisions consisted of bread and dried fish. A heavy rain which fell during the first few days of our journey soaked the loads of the pack-horses and caused the provisions to rot. . . . Meanwhile the cold was increasing day by day, and haste was necessary if we were to reach Verkhne-Kolymsk before the closing of the river. Therefore I left three Yakut with the horses and the goods, and prepared to descend the river on a raft with the rest of my party, hoping thus to reach a camp of the Yukaghir which is located on the course of the Korkodon.

It took us one day to build a strong raft, and then we began the descent of the river, made dangerous by numerous rapids and short bends, by the rocky banks and by jams of driftwood. Our guides had intimated that we could make the descent in two days, but instead we spent nine days on the raft.

Borgoras visited the extreme northeastern parts of Siberia and the Kamchatka Peninsula, the least Russianized areas of Siberia. Using as a base a little outpost at the mouth of the Anadyr River, which marked the furthest expansion of the Russians and Cossacks into Siberia at that time, Borgoras made extensive excursions into unexplored country, including some areas that were unknown even to his Siberian guides.

In 1903 the Jesup North Pacific Expedition officially came to an end. Jesup and the anthropological community believed a question had been settled—the Indians of the Americas had originally migrated from Siberia to the New World. But Boas was not finished. His broader goal had not been reached. Although the end of the expedition

The Central Asiatic Expedition's camel caravan crosses the desolate wastes of Tsagan Nor Valley in Outer Mongolia. This is one of a famous series of photographs carefully arranged by expedition leader Roy Chapman Andrews. (J.B. Shackelford, 1925)

resulted in reduced funds to work with, Boas instructed Laufer to remain in Asia and continue his work in Manchuria. Laufer kept a continuous stream of extraordinary material flowing into the museum's crowded storage rooms—clothes, food, the contents of Chinese pharmacies, blocks of tea, sake bowls, carved moustache sticks, shaman's rattles, powdered "dragon" bones, toys, and everything else that time and money allowed. The museum administration, especially the newly installed director Hermon C. Bumpus, watched Laufer's activity with mounting alarm. They saw precious storage space filling up with specimens that to them had little value, and finally they protested. Boas, a man not given to compromise, was angered at what he saw as interference with his curatorial activities, and he resigned from the museum.

Boas left behind the greatest collection of northeastern Asian ethnography in the world. He had been right: the museum had gone to Asia just in time. World War I, the Russian Revolution, disease, American whaling, and the spread of Western culture and Christianity contributed to the rapid extinction, or Westernization, of most of the aboriginal cultures of the circum-Pacific.

The end of the Jesup North Pacific Expedition was followed by a period of work in purely American anthropology. During this time, however, the seeds of a new era of Asian exploration were starting to sprout. In 1906 Roy Chapman Andrews, fresh from college, got his first job scrubbing floors in the taxidermy department of the museum. After seven months, he tagged along on a trip to Long Island to pick up a 54-foot North Atlantic right whale that had washed up dead on the beach. This trip sparked Andrews's interest in whales, which grew to the point where the museum sent him on several expeditions collecting and studying whales to British Columbia, Alaska, and finally to Japan and Korea. On his trips to the East he took photographs of Japanese and Korean scenery and people, which he had made into handcolored lantern slides for popular, "travelogue" lectures. The photographs in this book taken by Roy Chapman Andrews from 1908 to 1915 were from these trips. Gradually his interest began to shift from whales to Asia.

Andrews became interested in a theory, advanced by Henry Fairfield Osborn, then the museum's president, that Central Asia would turn out to be the birthplace of the human race. Since little or no hard scientific evidence supported the theory, Osborn had not found much enthusiasm for it among the paleontological community. Andrews felt differently. That the vast wastelands of the Gobi Desert—the stronghold of Genghis Khan—might contain the secret of human evolution appealed to his sense of adventure. And it was not a totally speculative theory, since the great civilizations of antiquity— China, India, the Near East—all formed a semicircle around Mongolia. Andrews and

The discovery of dinosaur eggs by the Central Asiatic Expedition in 1922 made front-page headlines throughout the world and electrified the scientific community. Here expedition leader Roy Chapman Andrews poses with "an even dozen" discovered in a nest in 1925. (J.B. Shackelford, 1925)

247

Osborn also believed, with much sounder reasoning, that the Gobi might contain abundant fossil evidence of early mammals.

In 1915 Andrews began planning the Central Asiatic Expedition. After several reconnaissance trips, the first leg of the expedition gathered in Peking in 1922 and set out beyond the Great Wall for Outer Mongolia in a fleet of motorcars and a caravan of 125 camels. Unlike the Jesup expedition, where anthropologists explored in small groups, Andrews had enlisted an army of people, including paleontologists, paleobotanists, archeologists, zoologists, geologists, topographers, medical doctors, photographers, guides, and for a short period the French Jesuit priest Teilhard de Chardin.

Andrews was a roughrider in the Teddy Roosevelt tradition, packing a revolver and wearing a cartridge belt of bullets around his waist. He had an excellent sense of publicity, and his photographer, J. B. Shackelford, was chosen as much for his abilities to take a dramatic picture as for his scientific qualifications. They spent hours arranging spectacular photographs of themselves: the camel caravan winding along the dunes of Tsagan Nor, Andrews climbing a precipice to an eagle's eyrie, and Andrews handling the first dinosaur egg—a picture that hit the front pages of newspapers across the United States. Walter Granger, the expedition's paleontologist, also had an interest in photography, as did Andrews. They took photographs of Chinese and Mongolians, with Andrews supplying copious and often inaccurate ethnographic notes. They were not anthropologists, and their interest was primarily in the curious, the foreign, the unusual, and the dramatic. Traversing Asia off and on for nearly a decade, they never did find evidence of early man in Central Asia, but they made important and spectacular discoveries of mammalian and dinosaurian fossils, as well as collecting extensive archeological and some ethnographic material.

Political problems in China brought the Central Asiatic Expedition to an end. When the Nationalist Party assumed control of a large part of China in 1928, antiforeign feeling was running high. A provincial governor seized part of the expedition's collections, which were released only after six weeks of negotiations. In 1930 the museum decided that further expeditions would meet with such opposition in China that they were out of the question, and Andrews was instructed to close his headquarters in Peking.

The immense collections of fossils brought back from Asia are still being studied. Some remain in a storage room in the museum's basement, still crated and encased in plaster, waiting for the time and money to open them up. The photographs, however, were immediately available and served to popularize the expedition and make Andrews famous.

The fruits of the Jesup North Pacific Expedition and the Central Asiatic Expedition are the backbone of the museum's Asian collections. But these were not the only expeditions to Asia sponsored by the museum. During the twenties and thirties, several wealthy friends of the museum offered their services mostly to collect animals for habitat groups. Sometimes these philanthropists were accompanied by museum scientists, but more often they traveled alone or in small parties.

The Vernay-Faunthorpe Expedition of 1923 was launched to India and Burma to collect rare animals for a proposed hall of Asiatic mammals. Arthur S. Vernay and Lieut.

Col. J. C. Faunthorpe were both British and very much men of the Empire—wealthy, upper-class, and the Asian equivalent of the "great white hunter." They took along cameras to photograph their adventures, but they also snapped rare pictures of Indian and Burmese life, some of which are reproduced in this book.

The Morden-Clark Expedition was led by Lieut. Col. William J. Morden and a museum preparator, James L. Clark. They explored the remote areas of the Himalayan plateau with guides and a caravan of yaks. Morden was an enthusiastic hunter, and his connection with the museum allowed him to stalk some of the most elusive big game in the world, including the long-haired Siberian tiger and the Marco Polo sheep. Morden and Clark, like Vernay and Faunthorpe, were not anthropologists, but they did take photographs of the people they encountered. Another philanthropist and collector, C. Suydam Cutting, a museum trustee, traveled extensively in Tibet, and was allegedly the first white Christian to enter the sacred city of Lhasa and gaze upon Potala, the great palace of the Dalai Lama. To gain the privilege, he had sent the Dalai Lama gold watches, fine hunting dogs, and electrical appliances.

The 1930s saw the "golden age" of museum expeditions draw to a close. Grand excursions were simply too expensive, and growing political problems were making collecting in many areas difficult if not impossible. In addition, the museum had greatly expanded its scope in the first quarter of the twentieth century, and anthropology had to share reduced funds with such sciences as ichthyology, animal behavior, herpetology, and mineral sciences.

The museum's Asian collections continued to grow when in 1942 Harry Shapiro became chairman of the Department of Anthropology, and a new era of Asian study and collecting began. Shapiro took a long hard look at the museum's ethnographic collections and determined their weaknesses. Southeast Asia, Arabia, Turkey, Afghanistan, and Iran were all poorly represented. Major expeditions like the North Pacific and Central Asiatic were out of the question, while the haphazard acquisition of material by gift and purchase was also unsatisfactory. "I was impressed," says Shapiro, who is now curator emeritus, "by the rapid disappearance of many of the world's traditional cultures. There wasn't much time left—perhaps a few decades."

With his department's limited resources, he developed a plan. Whenever anthropologists went into the field to do research, Shapiro called them up. Would they be willing to collect for the museum? By carefully targeting specific areas of Asia, he was able to develop very fine collections in numerous areas, such as the superb Dentan collection of Senoi-Semai artifacts from Malaysia, the Louis Dupree collection from Afghanistan, the Krader collection from Iran, and the Kenan Erin collection from Turkey; private collectors added many rare and beautiful works of art in areas not covered by museum anthropologists.

The museum's Asian collection could not be duplicated today. It is a priceless record of the traditional cultures of Asia before they were destroyed or changed by the modern era. And even more than that, it is a testament to the richness, the infinite variety, and the achievement of the human spirit.

BIBLIOGRAPHY

CHAPTER I

Bowles, Gordon T. *The People of Asia*. New York: Scribner's, 1978

Cressey, George B. *Asia's Land and People*. 3rd ed. New York: McGraw-Hill, 1963

Dudley, Guilford A. *A History of Eastern Civilizations*. New York: Wiley, 1973

Latham, Ronald (tr.). *The Travels of Marco Polo*. Penguin Books, 1958

Myrdal, Gunnar. *Asian Drama: An Inquiry into the Poverty of Nations*. One-vol. abridged (Seth King, ed.). New York: Pantheon, 1972

Parrinder, Geoffrey. *Introduction to Asian Religions*. Oxford and New York: Oxford University Press, 1976

Shaplen, Robert. *A Turning Wheel: Three Decades of the Asian Revolution as Witnessed by a Correspondent for the New Yorker*. New York: Random House, 1979

Simkin, C. G. *Traditional Trade of Asia*. Oxford and New York: Oxford University Press, 1968

Steadmen, John A. *The Myth of Asia*. New York: Simon & Schuster, 1969

Welty, Paul T. *The Asians: Their Heritage and Their Destiny*. 5th ed. New York: Harper & Row, 1976

CHAPTER II

Ardrey, Robert. *African Genesis*. New York: Atheneum, 1973

Braidwood, Robert J. *Prehistoric Men*. 8th ed. Glenview, Ill.: Scott, Foresman, 1975

Hawkes, Jaquetta. *Atlas of Early Man*. New York: St. Martin's, 1976

Hilger, M. Inex. *Together with the Ainu: A Vanishing People*. Norman: University of Oklahoma Press, 1971

Kramer, Samuel N. *The Sumerians: Their History, Culture, and Character*. Chicago: University of Chicago Press, 1971

Leakey, Richard, and Lewin, Roger. *Origins: What New Discoveries Reveal about the Emergence of Our Species and Its Possible Future*. New York: Dutton, 1977

Shapiro, Harry. *Peking Man*. New York: Simon & Schuster, 1977

Starr, Chester G. *Early Man: Prehistory and the Civilizations of the Ancient Near East*. Oxford and New York: Oxford University Press, 1973

Von Koenigswald, G. H. *The Evolution of Man*. Rev. ed. Ann Arbor: University of Michigan Press, 1976

Weidenreich, Franz. *Apes, Giants, and Man*. Chicago: University of Chicago Press, 1946

CHAPTER III

Fisher, Sydney N. *The Middle East: A History*. 3rd ed. New York: Knopf, 1978

Fox, Robin L. *The Search for Alexander*. Boston: Little, Brown, 1980

Guillaume, Alfred. *Islam*. Penguin Books, 1954

Johnson, Paul. *Civilizations of the Holy Land*. New York: Atheneum, 1979

Kinross, Lord. *The Ottoman Centuries: The Rise and Fall of the Turkish Empire*. New York: Morrow, 1979

Nasr, Seyyed H. *Ideals and Realities of Islam*. Boston: Beacon Press, 1972

Oppenheim, A. Leo. *Ancient Mesopotamia: Portrait of a Dead Civilization*. Rev. ed. Chicago: University of Chicago Press, 1976

Oriental Institute. *The 1919-20 Breasted Expedition to the Near East*. Chicago: University of Chicago Press, 1977

Schacht, Joseph, and Bosworth, C. E. (eds.). *The Legacy of Islam*. 2nd ed. Oxford and New York: Oxford University Press, 1979

CHAPTER IV

Allchin, B. and R. *The Birth of Indian Civilization, India and Pakistan Before 500 B.C.* Penguin Books, 1968

Auboyer, Jeanine. *Daily Life in Ancient India*. New York: Macmillan, 1965

Basham, A. L. *A Cultural History of India*. Oxford and New York: Oxford University Press, 1975

Bayley, Emily, and Metcalfe, Thomas. *The Golden Calm*. New York: Viking, 1980

Conze, Edward. *Buddhist Thought in India*. Ann Arbor: University of Michigan Press, 1967

Godden, Jon, and Godden, Rumer. *Shiva's Pigeons: An Experience of India*. New York: Viking, 1972

Golant, William. *The Long Afternoon: British India 1607-1947*. New York: St. Martin's, 1975

Hutton, John H. *Caste in India: Its Nature, Function, and Origins*. 4th ed. Oxford and New York: Oxford University Press, 1963

Mehta, Ved. *Mahatma Gandhi and His Apostles*. Penguin Books, 1977

Naipaul, V. S. *India: A Wounded Civilization*. New York: Knopf, 1977

Srinivas, M. N. *The Remembered Village*. Berkeley: University of California Press, 1977

Wheeler, Mortimer. *Indus Civilization*. 3rd ed. Cambridge University Press, 1968

Zaehner, R. C. (ed.). *Hindu Scriptures*. New York: Dutton, 1976

CHAPTER V

Arnold, Eve. *In China*. New York: Knopf, 1980

Blofeld, John. *Taoism: The Road to Immortality*. Boulder: Shambhala, 1979

Bloodworth, Denis. *The Chinese Looking Glass*. Rev. ed. New York: Farrar, Straus, 1980

Chen, Jack. *The Chinese of America*. New York: Harper & Row, 1980

Cohen, Joan Lebold, and Cohen, Jerome Alan. *China Today and Her Ancient Treasures*. 2nd ed. New York: Abrams, 1980

Dawson, Raymond. *The Chinese Experience*. New York: Scribner's, 1978

Dun, J. Li. *The Ageless Chinese: A History*. 2nd ed. New York: Scribner's 1971

Fong, Wen (ed.). *The Great Bronze Age in China*. New York: Knopf, 1980

McNaughton, William (ed.). *The Confucian Vision*. Ann Arbor: University of Michigan Press, 1974

Meskill, John (ed.). *An Introduction to Chinese Civilization*. New York: Columbia University Press, 1973

Myrdal, Jan. *Report from a Chinese Village*. New York: Pantheon, 1965

Rawson, Jessica. *Ancient China: Art and Archeology*. New York: Harper & Row, 1980

Wilhelm, Hellmut. *Change: Eight Lectures on the I Ching*. Princeton University Press, 1960

CHAPTER VI

Benedict, Ruth. *The Chrysanthemum and the Sword*. New York: New American Library, 1967

Dore, Ronald P. *Shinohata: Portrait of a Japanese Village*. New York: Pantheon, 1980

Hori, Ichiro. *Folk Religion in Japan; Continuity and Change*. Chicago: University of Chicago Press, 1974

Morris, Ivan. *The World of the Shining Prince: Court Life in Ancient Japan*. Penguin Books, 1979

Reischauer, Edwin O. *The Japanese*. Cambridge: Harvard University Press, 1977

Sansom, G. B. *Japan: A Short Cultural History*. Palo Alto: Stanford University Press, 1978

Sen, Soshitsu. *Chado: The Japanese Way of Tea*. New York: Weatherhill, 1979

Suzuki, Daisetz T. *Zen and Japanese Culture*. Princeton University Press, 1959

Toynbee, Arnold, et. al. *Introducing Japan*. New York: St. Martin's, 1978

Yee, Chiang. *The Silent Traveller in Japan*. New York: Norton, 1972

CHAPTER VII

Blunt, Wilfrid. *The Golden Road to Samarkand*. New York: Viking, 1975

DeBary, William T. (ed.). *The Buddhist Tradition: In India, China, and Japan*. New York: Random House, 1972

Dupree, Louis. *Afghanistan*. Princeton University Press, 1973

Harrison, Brian. *Southeast Asia: A Short History*. 3rd ed. New York: St. Martin's, 1968

Lattimore, Owen and Eleanor (eds.). *Silks, Spices and Empire: Asia Seen Through the Eyes of Its Discoverers*. New York: Delacorte, 1968

Mowat, Farley. *The Siberians*. Penguin Books, 1972

Myrdal, Jan. *The Silk Road: A Journey from the High Pamirs and Ili Through Sinkiang and Kansu*. New York: Pantheon, 1980

Snellgrove, David, and Richardson, Hugh. *A Cultural History of Tibet*. New York: Praeger, 1968

Theroux, Paul. *The Great Railway Bazaar: By Train Through Asia*. Boston: Houghton Mifflin, 1975

CREDITS

All objects and photographs in this book are in the collection of the American Museum of Natural History, New York City.

Pages 2–3: Gurnee Dyer photo; *4–5*: hand-colored lantern slide; *6–7*: Gurnee Dyer photo; *8–9*: hand-colored lantern slide; *10–11*: J. Stefanik photo; *12–13*: hand-colored lantern slide; *14–15*: hand-colored lantern slide; *33*: Gift of William B. Whitney, 70.0/7481; *34*: Gift of W.L. Hildburgh, 70.0/1985; *35*: Gift of Benjamin Moore, 70.0/3361; *36*: 70.2/866; *37*: Gift of William B. Whitney, 70.0/7187; *38*: Gift of W.L. Hildburgh, 70.0/4416; *39*: Gift of William B. Whitney, 70.0/7545 (*left*), 70.0/7463 (*right*); *40*: Gift of William B. Whitney, 70.0/7431; *57*: cast of skull XI, 99.1/2180; *58*: Gift of Gertrude Hickman Thompson, 73/3245; *59*: Gift of Gertrude Hickman Thompson, 73/3165; *60*: 73/3819; *61*: Gift of Gilbert W. Kahn, Roger W. Kahn, Mrs. John Barry Ryan, Jr., Lady Maud Marriott, 73/3429; *62*: Gift of Gilbert W. Kahn, Roger W. Kahn, Mrs. John Barry Ryan, Jr., Lady Maud Marriott, 73/3428; *63*: Gift of W.L. Hildburgh, 70.0/4356 *64*: 70.3/2435 (*left*), 70.3/2436 (*right*); *65*: 70.2/773; *66*: 70.0/ 250; *67*: Gift of Lester Wolfe, 70.2/2200, 2199; 70.2/6982, 3086, 7000, 6985, 6987, 4673, 6986, 6984; *68*: 70.2/

3759;*85*: Gift of the Kingdom of Saudi Arabia, Ministry of Education, 70.3/993 (*left*), 70.2/6420 (*center*), 70.2/8537 (*right*); *86*: Gift of Julius Kushner, 70.3/ 2488 (*Torah*); Gift of Mount Neboh Congregation and the Union of American Hebrew Congregations, 70.3/2483 (*crowns*); *87*: 70.3/2752 (*stand*), 70.2/7699 (*vessel*); *88*: 70.2/ 5301; *89*: 70.3/2318 (*top*), 70.3/ 2392 (*bottom*); *90*: 70.2/4615; *91*: Gift of Mr. & Mrs. Boghos Derghazarian, 70.3/2836 (*belt*); Gift of Mrs. Veronica A. Leylekian, 70.3/2890 (*tray*); *92*: 70.2/4841; *93*: 70.3/2334; *94*: Gift of Mr. & Mrs. John P. Young, 70.2/8582; *95*: 70.3/2327; *96*: 70.2/6993; *129*:70.2/7867; *130*: Gift of H.L. Shapiro, 70.2/5256 (*left*), 70.2/5258, (*right*); *131*: 70.2/8017; *132*: Gift of Mr. & Mrs. W. Gurnee Dyer, 70.2/5270; *133*: American Museum of Natural History photo, 70.3/1583; *135*: 70.2/7820; *134*: 70.2/8573; *136*: Gift of W.L. Hildburgh, 70.0/4727; *137*: 70.2/380; *138*: 70.2/8016; *139*: 70.2/ 8018 (*left*), 70.2/8019 (*right*); *140*: Albert Rudolph and Ray Rudolph from the Rudolph family, 70.3/1581; *157*: Laufer Collection, 70/14639; *158*: Gift of Isaac Wyman Drummond, 70.3/1883, 1960, 2024, 1944, 2154, 1940, 1914, 1836, 1972, 2134, 2063; *159*: Gift of Isaac Wyman Drummond, 70.3/2541; *166–7*: Gift of Holbrook Blinn, 70.0/3584; *162*:

Laufer Collection, 70/10879; *163*: Gift of Isaac Wyman Drummond, 70.3/2659; *164*: Laufer Collection, 70/11750; *165*: Gift of Gilbert W. Kahn, Roger W. Kahn, Mrs. John Barry Ryan, Jr., Lady Maud Marriot, 73/7276, 7277; *160*: 70.3/2420; *161*: Laufer Collection, 70/14708, 14709; *168*: Gift of Antoinette K. Gordon, 70.0/7728; *185*: Gift of Kenneth Heuer, 70.2/5408; *186*: Gift of Antoinette K. Gordon, 70.3/4146; *187*: Gift of Alice Baker, 70.3/2426; *188*: Gift of George D. Pratt, 73/439; *189*: Gift of W.L. Hildburgh, 70.0/3644; *190*: Gift of W.L. Hildburgh, 70.0/3633; *191*: Gift of Isaac Wyman Drummond, 70.3/655; *192*: Gift of Isaac Wyman Drummond, 70.3/809; *193*: Gift of Isaac Wyman Drummond, 70.3/819; *194*: Gift of Isaac Wyman Drummond, 70.3/616; *195*: Gift of Isaac Wyman Drummond, 70.3/577; *196*: Gift of Isaac Wyman Drummond, 70.3/812; *213*: 70.3/4147; *214*: Gift of J.G. Phelps Stokes, 70.0/139; *215*: 70.0/8490 (*skirt*), 70.0/8456 (*hat*), 70.0/8459 (*belt*), 70.0/8457 (*coat*); *216*: Laufer Collection, 70/702; *217*: Gift of Antoinette K. Gordon, 70.3/1386; *218*: Jochelson Collection, 70/8711; *219*: Bogoras Collection, 70/7174; *220*: Jochelson Collection, 70/9072; *221*: Laufer Collection, 70/625; *222*: Jochelson Collection, 70/8488; *223*: Bogoras Collection, 70/7331; *224*: Bogoras Collection, 70/6397

INDEX